HEALTH REPORTS:
DISEASES AND DISORDERS

ASTHMA

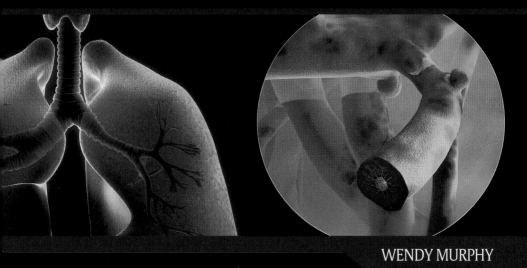

WENDY MURPHY

TWENTY-FIRST CENTURY BOOKS
MINNEAPOLIS

Twenty-First Century Books
A division of Lerner Publishing Group, Inc.
241 First Avenue North
Minneapolis, MN 55401 U.S.A.

Website address: www.lernerbooks.com

Library of Congress Cataloging-in-Publication Data

Murphy, Wendy B.
     Asthma / by Wendy Murphy.
         p.   cm. — (USA today health reports. Diseases and disorders)
     Includes bibliographical references and index.
     ISBN 978-0-7613-5457-4 (lib. bdg. : alk. paper)
     1. Asthma—Popular works. I. Title.
     RC591.M862 2011
     616.2'38—dc22   2010033947

Manufactured in the United States of America
1 – DP – 12/31/10

CONTENTS

USA TODAY
HEALTH REPORTS:
DISEASES AND DISORDERS

CHAPTER ONE

ASTHMA BASICS

To most people, George seemed like a typical thirteen-year-old student. He didn't mind most subjects in school, enjoyed video games, and loved playing a variety of sports. But for as long as he could remember, George had to be careful about his daily activities because of his asthma. As a young boy, he used to wake up in the middle of the night wheezing and coughing. One night his coughing attack was so bad that his parents brought him to the hospital emergency room. The doctors at the hospital gave George special medication that helped him breathe more easily. They told his parents that George should see a pulmonologist and an allergist—these types of doctors specialize in breathing problems and allergies. The doctors did a range of tests and determined that George had asthma and was allergic to many things, including dust, mold, pet dander, and pollen.

After the asthma diagnosis, George and his family were more aware of how his activities and environment affected his asthma. They asked the doctor many questions and did a lot of research. They found many different ways to help treat and control George's asthma. They cleaned the carpeting in the house thoroughly and even removed it in some rooms. The family dog wasn't allowed to sleep in George's bed anymore. The whole family was more diligent about cleaning, vacuuming, and dusting around the house.

George also learned about what he could do every day to stay healthy. The allergist prescribed medication for George to take on a daily basis to prevent asthma attacks. Emergency asthma medication was always nearby in case George needed it. George can't help that he has asthma, but he doesn't let it stop him from living an active and happy life.

AN IRRITATING DISEASE

Asthma, or bronchial asthma as it is also called, is a chronic disease of the lungs. A chronic disease has no permanent cure. Its underlying causes in the body are not going to go away. Asthma is not contagious. You can't catch asthma from someone who has it. Asthma can be mild, or it can severely affect people. But asthma is generally very controllable when it is fully understood. If you or someone you know has asthma, you can get to know the disease, learn how to deal with it, and then go about enjoying your life.

Asthma mostly affects breathing. Most young people with asthma are able to breathe normally most of the time. Asthma attacks can occur as often as several times a day or as infrequently as once a month or even less. During an asthma attack, a person finds it very difficult to take air in and out of the lungs. The lining of tubes that carry air between the throat and lungs becomes swollen. The airways partially close. These reactions are the result of coming into

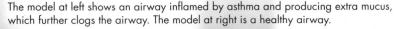

The model at left shows an airway inflamed by asthma and producing extra mucus, which further clogs the airway. The model at right is a healthy airway.

Exposure to pet dander is a major trigger of asthma attacks in humans. If a family has a dog or a cat, they must vacuum regularly to clear the house of dander and other asthma triggers.

contact with some type of irritant. The irritant is usually airborne, such as dust or animal dander in the air. Symptoms of asthma can also be triggered by a chemical smell, a food or food ingredient, or even a blast of winter wind.

When exposed to the irritant, the person with asthma may start wheezing and gasping for air. One young asthma patient says that during an asthma attack, breathing feels "like trying to suck peanut butter through a soda straw." Others compare severe asthma attacks to the sensation of having a full-grown man standing on their chest, or feeling like they are slowly drowning. The chest becomes uncomfortably tight, as though it's been wound with rubber bands. These can be scary experiences for a young person with asthma and for everyone around him or her. It doesn't help that people who don't know what to do tend to overreact or panic during an attack.

Fortunately, well-informed people can do a lot to reduce the frequency of episodes like this. And when one does occur, they can act in ways that bring relief.

WHO HAS ASTHMA?

Many people live with asthma. In fact, as of 2011, about twenty-three million Americans are dealing with the disease. Asthma usually first appears during childhood, and it is the most common serious chronic disease among children in the United States. It affects nearly seven million people under the age of eighteen. Young boys with asthma outnumber young girls. But the balance begins to swing in the opposite direction as girls and boys grow up. At that point, more young women than young men have asthma.

Asthma is near the top of the list of conditions that send children to hospital emergency rooms. The disease may also require them to stay in hospitals for extended periods for observation and treatment.

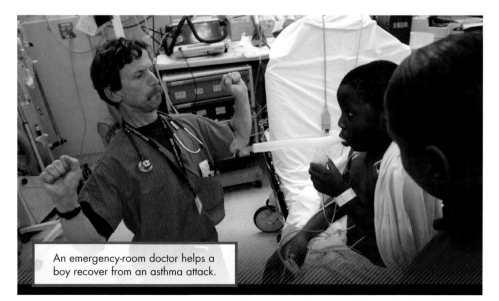

An emergency-room doctor helps a boy recover from an asthma attack.

USA TODAY Snapshots®

What are the most costly medical ailments in children?

Nearly $100 billion was spent to treat medical problems in children ages 17 and under in 2006[1]. The three most expensive: (in billions)

Mental disorders — **$8.9**

Asthma — **$8.0**

Trauma disorders (including fractures, sprains, burns) — **$6.1**

1 – The most recent year data was available
Source: Agency for Healthcare Research and Quality, 2009

By Michelle Healy and Sam Ward, USA TODAY, 2009

This is because it can take time for parents, doctors, and the children involved to learn to control this disease. In total, children miss almost thirteen million school days a year because of asthma. This makes it the leading cause of absenteeism in school. All these factors make asthma very costly to the United States. The U.S. government spends billions of dollars on treatment and research relating to asthma.

Most young people who develop asthma begin to show symptoms before their fifth birthdays. A small minority develops symptoms of asthma while they're still babies. The first asthma episode is often connected with some other severe but short-term respiratory illnesses such as the flu, bronchitis, or pneumonia. These sicknesses provide the opportunity for asthma to show itself. The asthma was most likely present all along but was waiting for the right set of circumstances to turn on. Some people may not know they have asthma until they reach their teen years. They may have been misdiagnosed years before as having chronic bronchitis, only to find out that they actually have asthma. It's possible for adults to have a first bout of asthma in their thirties or forties or even later.

The number of cases of asthma among people of all ages is rising quickly. The growing statistics are especially noticeable among youngsters living in the inner city. This puts children in low-income groups, which include a higher percentage of African Americans and Hispanics, at higher risk. These kids are more likely to live in poor, urban neighborhoods. No one knows precisely why these changes are occurring. One likely reason is that people's lifestyles and surroundings have altered in recent years. Many children of the twenty-first century, for instance, spend more hours indoors than earlier generations did. Hanging around the house watching TV or playing video games for long periods of time exposes a child's lungs to more of the substances that trigger asthma. Improved insulation that has made houses warmer in winter is another likely reason for more asthma. The drafts that made old houses hard to heat also helped to keep the air inside fresh. The air in more tightly insulated modern houses does not mix as much with outside air, so it is not as fresh.

Besides environmental factors, the physical risks of spending too much time sitting indoors may also account for the rise in asthma rates. Less physical activity and unhealthy diets are causing an increase in childhood obesity.

Spending too much time indoors can increase children's exposure to asthma-triggering substances. Researchers also think that lack of exercise increases the chances of childhood asthma.

www.usatoday.com

USA TODAY

Life

SECTION D

May 12, 2010

From the Pages of USA TODAY

Reversing childhood obesity

Restaurants need to offer healthier choices on children's menus. The food and beverage industry should market nutritious foods, not junk foods, to kids. And families should eat dinner together as often as possible.

Schools need to make sure elementary students get recess, and the federal government needs to improve the nutritional quality of food commodities provided to schools.

These are among a federal task force's wide-ranging recommendations to reverse childhood obesity. It was released Tuesday by first lady Michelle Obama.

"For the first time, the nation will have goals, benchmarks and measureable outcomes that will help us tackle the childhood obesity epidemic one child, one family and one community at a time," she said.

Solve the problem in a generation

The goal of the plan is to try to solve childhood obesity in a generation, the report says. That means returning to a childhood obesity rate of 5% by 2030. Right now, about 32% of children and adolescents today—25 million young people—are obese or overweight, government statistics show.

Those extra pounds put children at a greater risk of developing a host of debilitating and costly diseases, including type 2 diabetes, high blood pressure and high cholesterol. And children today may lead shorter lives by two to five years than their parents because of obesity, a 2005 study found.

Government agencies are already working to get healthier foods in schools, expand physical activity in schools and provide mothers with better prenatal care, the first lady said.

To prepare the report, which was requested by President Obama, the task force reviewed research, consulted with experts, considered 2,500 comments from the public and consulted 12 federal agencies, including the Departments of Agriculture, Defense, Education and Health and Human Services.

Among the recommendations:

- Restaurants should consider their portion sizes and improve children's menus.
- The food and beverage industry should develop aggressive targets for increasing the proportion of advertisements for healthy foods and beverages. Within three years, the majority of food and beverage ads directed to children should promote healthy foods.

Eating a healthy, balanced diet is key to avoiding childhood obesity. The U.S. government is working with schools to try to provide more nutritious food for school lunches *(above)*.

- Media and entertainment companies should limit licensing of their popular characters to healthy food and beverage products.
- Local governments should create incentives to attract supermarkets and grocery stores to underserved neighborhoods.
- The federal government should provide economic incentives to increase production of healthy foods such as fruits, vegetables and whole grains.
- Government, businesses and foundations should work to increase the number of safe parks and playgrounds, particularly in underserved and low-income communities.
- The federal government, working with local communities, should distribute information about the upcoming 2010 Dietary Guidelines for Americans through simple messages, such as: Drink water instead of soda or juice with added sugar; eat more fruits, vegetables, whole grains, and lean proteins; choose low-fat or fat-free dairy products; and, when possible, eat dinner together as a family.

Earning praise from experts

The recommendations are drawing applause from childhood obesity specialists. "It's very comprehensive with lots of detailed recommendations that could make a real dent in childhood obesity," says Margo Wootan, director of nutrition policy for the Center for Science in the Public Interest, a Washington-D.C.-based consumer group.

"It lays out steps that the federal government, schools, parents and food companies can take. These are not pie-in-the-sky recommendations. They are doable."

—*Nanci Hellmich*

An obese person is extremely over-weight. Scientists are finding connections between childhood obesity and asthma. Studies have shown that obesity appears to be a risk factor for developing asthma. This means that a person who is obese may be more likely to develop asthma. An obese person's extra weight may cause the airways to narrow, making it harder to breathe.

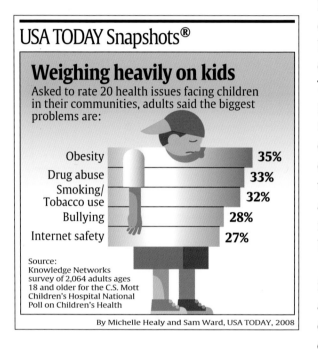

USA TODAY Snapshots®

Weighing heavily on kids

Asked to rate 20 health issues facing children in their communities, adults said the biggest problems are:

Obesity — **35%**
Drug abuse — **33%**
Smoking/Tobacco use — **32%**
Bullying — **28%**
Internet safety — **27%**

Source: Knowledge Networks survey of 2,064 adults ages 18 and older for the C.S. Mott Children's Hospital National Poll on Children's Health

By Michelle Healy and Sam Ward, USA TODAY, 2008

Still another factor in rising rates of asthma may be the drop in other kinds of childhood infections. More U.S. children are immunized—protected by vaccines—at an early age. The vaccines protect children against infections that may once have made people less vulnerable to allergies. And allergies have become one of the prime causes of asthma.

Some hereditary factors also contribute to the likelihood of developing asthma. The majority of young people who develop asthma can trace a family history of asthma or to some other allergic condition. These conditions can include hay fever or eczema (a bad skin rash). Inheriting a tendency toward asthma works much the way inheriting eye color or height does. A child with one asthmatic parent is three to six times as likely to contract asthma as a child with no family history of allergies. If both parents have asthma, the risk is ten times greater.

Other factors that can bring on asthma are a major viral infection, which can be caused by the influenza or cold viruses, or long-term exposure to some kinds of severe air pollution. Researchers have noticed, for example, that asthma is less prevalent in those parts of the world where there is no industrial development, no air pollution or widespread use of synthetic chemicals, and where people live in much the same way as their ancestors lived hundreds of years ago. Some asthma specialists have gone so far as to declare asthma a disease of industrialized civilizations.

Air pollution is another trigger of asthma. Cities with high levels of airborne pollution, such as Los Angeles, California *(shown below)*, have high levels of asthma among the population.

www.usatoday.com

USA TODAY

News
SECTION A

March 24, 2010

From the Pages of USA TODAY

Measures across U.S. target port pollution

Joe Johnson isn't a scientist, but he knows that the giant, smoke-spewing ships that dock at the Port of Baltimore [Maryland] can't be good for his health—or that of his 9-year-old son. "Those things just look evil," says Johnson, a handyman who lives in a row house just east of the port. "When the wind blows the wrong way, there's no telling what kind of [pollutants] we're breathing."

Approximately 87 million Americans who live near major seaports are breathing some of the nation's dirtiest—and most dangerous—air, the Environmental Protection Agency [EPA] says. But help is on the way, thanks to initiatives across the USA to cut pollution coming from ships, vehicles and other sources within the ports themselves.

"We're trying to be creative, and we're getting a lot of help from the government," says Richard Sheckells Jr., chief of environmental initiatives for the Maryland Port Administration.

Dirty emissions from ships, trucks, and facilities at U.S. ports contribute to air pollution, which is linked to high rates of asthma in the communities nearby.

Baltimore port officials are using federal stimulus money to help companies retrofit tugboats and other vehicles with cleaner engines. Ports in California, New Jersey and elsewhere are spending more than $100 million in public and private funds to help replace aging trucks with newer, less polluting vehicles.

Communities near ports tend to suffer from above-average rates of cancer and asthma, according to EPA head Lisa Jackson. Jackson has estimated that 40 of the largest 100 U.S. ports are located in metropolitan areas that fail to meet federal air-quality standards.

A 2007 study published by the American Chemical Society estimated that, worldwide, pollution from ocean-going ships causes about 60,000 premature deaths a year from heart and lung cancers and other ailments.

Environmental problems at ports "flew under the radar" until just a few years ago, says Elena Craft of the Environmental Defense Fund, a non-profit group. She says a series of lawsuits and petitions by community and environmental groups, especially in California, helped persuade ports and cargo companies to act. Some of the measures have been controversial. More than 100 truckers staged a November protest in Los Angeles [California] to demand more time to meet new pollution standards.

The Obama administration has also been more active than its predecessors in both enforcing environmental regulations and in providing federal stimulus funds and other aid to help upgrade equipment, says Mike Reagoso, vice president of McAllister Towing, which operates vessels in Baltimore and elsewhere.

Among other steps:

- The Port of Los Angeles plans to begin using 20 new electric-powered trucks this spring, Knatz says. Other new vehicles have already helped cut emissions by about 70% compared to 2005, she says.

- Since 2008, the Port of Baltimore has spent $272,000 retrofitting cranes and other equipment, Sheckells says. The port is also working on a project that would take waste produced from dredging and recycle it for use in road construction, he says.

- The Port Authority of New York and New Jersey said this month it and the EPA would provide $28 million in financing to help replace about 600 trucks made before 1993 in an effort to cut soot pollution by two-thirds.

The EPA estimates that shipping companies would, over time, need to spend about $3.2 billion to adapt to new rules. Some of that cost would trickle down to consumers. Jackson estimates that would, on average, add about three cents to a pair of sneakers made abroad and shipped into the USA.

"This is all a balancing act between cost and the environment," says Lorena Johnston of Vane Brothers, which operates tugs and barges on the East Coast. "But we're convinced it's the right thing to do."

—*Garrett Hubbard*

ANCIENT IDEAS

Though it was less common in past centuries, asthma has been around for a very long time. The ancient Greeks were the ones who gave asthma its name. Roughly translated, the word *asthma* means "panting." This is a pretty good way to describe the heavy, labored, rapid breathing that asthmatics experience when an acute (sudden) attack comes on.

Like most diseases, asthma wasn't well understood by ancient physicians and healers. It was easy for doctors to mistake asthma for other long-term lung diseases, which they also didn't understand. Another challenge for medical workers before the twentieth century was the lack of modern tools such as X-rays and breath-monitoring devices. These instruments allow doctors to see what is going on inside the lungs and throat during an asthma attack.

The best of the early medical workers noticed that some panting people also had allergic reactions to foods. But they blamed it on what they thought were poisons in the food. One of the many antidotes to these so-called poisons was offered in an old guide for English doctors. It recommended a potion of dried and crumbled foxes' lungs as a remedy for the breathing difficulties associated with asthma. As recently as 1910, cold baths, poultices (a soft mixture) of hot oatmeal, and medicines prepared from skunkweed and peppermint were suggested as powerful cures for asthma. These preparations most likely provided no help. In fact, they may have increased asthmatics' suffering.

Only in recent decades has a clear picture of asthma begun to appear. Since the 1980s, a wide range of asthma drugs has been developed. People who are experiencing asthma for the first time have the advantage of access to twenty-first-century medical knowledge.

ASTHMA AND THE LUNGS

Asthma attacks take place in the airways of the lungs. The lungs are the most important part of the human respiratory system. They consist of two inflatable sacs within the rib cage. The lungs regulate the amounts of oxygen and carbon dioxide gases in the blood. Air moves in and out with each breath. A complete exchange of old air for new air takes several breaths.

Normally, the breathing necessary to keep the body alive goes on automatically, without you being aware of it. The air you breathe enters your body through the nose and mouth. It travels first to the pharynx, a muscular part of your throat. Then it passes through your trachea, or windpipe. It is a fairly rigid tube that extends downward through the neck to the center of the chest, behind your heart. At the lower end of the windpipe, the trachea divides into two smaller bronchial tubes. Each tube enters a lung. A bronchial tube is structured like an upside-down tree. Its main trunk branches down and out into smaller bronchi and still-smaller tubes called bronchioles.

The entire length of the branching airways is lined with a delicate layer of cells known as the mucosa. These mucosal cells produce a sticky substance known as mucus. The mucus traps dust and other irritants. Under normal circumstances, the mucus carries the irritants up and out of the lungs to be swallowed or spit out through coughing. The mucus must keep moving in the right direction so that the airways stay open and unclogged. The smooth muscle walls of the bronchial tubes are lined with thousands of tiny, whiplike structures called cilia. The cilia wave back and forth like tiny brooms, pushing the dirty mucus upward toward the exits in the back of the mouth.

At the very end of the bronchial tree—at the tips of the finest branches—are tiny clusters of air sacs called alveoli. The lungs have about 300 million alveoli. They look like microscopic grapes or leaves. Scientists estimate that if they were opened up and spread out, the total area of the alveoli would be about 70 square meters, or roughly 753 square feet. Normally, the tiny sacs expand and contract steadily, inflating and deflating about fifteen to sixteen times a minute. With each breath, oxygen passes through the thin walls of the air sacs and enters the equally thin walls of the smallest blood vessels. These hair-like channels are known as capillaries. From there, blood transports oxygen throughout the body. It nourishes several hundred trillion specialized cells in our bodies. At the same time the oxygen enters the blood, carbon dioxide—a waste product of those same hardworking cells—passes into the alveoli to be exhaled, or breathed out.

The powerful breathing muscle known as the diaphragm keeps things moving along smoothly. The diaphragm is a large, dome-shaped muscle that provides a kind of floor between the chest cavity and the abdominal cavity below. In normal breathing, the diaphragm contracts as a person inhales. The ribs lift upward and the space within your chest cavity increases. The effect of this increasing space is to suck air in, filling the lungs with oxygen. When a person breathes out, the process reverses. The space in the chest cavity gets smaller, and pressure builds up against the inflated lungs. Air is squeezed out, taking the carbon dioxide waste with it.

ASTHMA ATTACKS

During an asthma episode, four things happen to interrupt the normal breathing process:

- the inner linings of the airways become inflamed and swollen
- the muscles around the large and small airways tighten
- the swollen and squeezed airways produce extra mucus, making the already narrowed passageways even more congested
- stale air becomes trapped in the alveoli

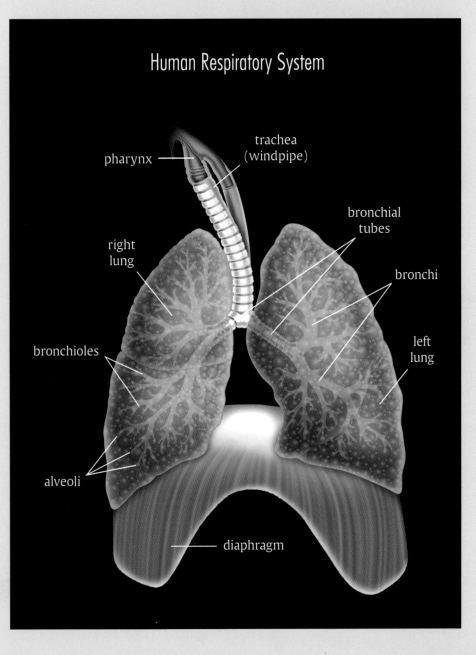

Human Respiratory System

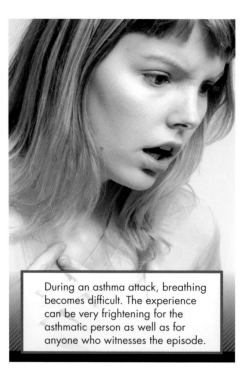

During an asthma attack, breathing becomes difficult. The experience can be very frightening for the asthmatic person as well as for anyone who witnesses the episode.

The frightening result is that breathing in and out becomes more difficult. An instinctive reaction is to gasp for more fresh, oxygen-rich air. A person in this situation finds that he or she can't take in enough air to restore a balance. Another natural reaction is to cough. This is an instinctive attempt to dislodge some of the extra mucus that is clogging the airways. The little air that does manage to move has to go through abnormally confined spaces, causing wheezing and whistling sounds.

Some asthmatic episodes are mild and last only a few minutes before normal breathing returns. But if an attack is severe and lasts for an extended period, the person may become pale and break out in a cold sweat. Fingertips and lips may turn bluish. This shows that the oxygen that normally keeps human blood a rich red color is in seriously short supply.

Anyone who experiences bronchial asthma has what doctors call "twitchy" lung tissue. This means the person with asthma has lungs that are uncommonly sensitive or react strongly to one or more factors. These factors, known as asthma triggers, vary widely in the asthmatic population. Some people with asthma are bothered by one trigger, while others are sensitive to many triggers. The degree to which people with asthma react to triggers can range from mild and infrequent to severe and daily.

ASTHMA, THE IMMUNE SYSTEM, AND ALLERGIES

By far the largest and most persistent category of triggers is allergic reactions. An allergy is usually defined as an exaggerated response to some substance. This reaction involves the body's immune system.

The immune system normally protects the body from invaders. When the immune system detects an infection or some other foreign substance that might cause harm, it produces chemical substances known as antibodies. Antibodies are like friendly soldiers that patrol the body looking for harmful substances, called antigens. The antibodies try to neutralize or destroy the antigens by releasing a variety of chemicals.

The immune system produces an antibody known as immunoglobulin E, or IgE. Whenever and wherever an IgE antibody finds a foreign invader, such as an allergenic (allergy-causing) substance, it latches on. Once in action, the IgE antibody calls for backup chemicals called histamines and leukotrienes. Histamines and leukotrienes irritate and inflame the cells. This causes swelling and fluid buildup. In an ideal situation, the immune system uses this swollen and watery environment to destroy the invading substance. A severe or extreme allergic reaction by the immune system is called anaphylaxis or anaphylactic shock. Anaphylaxis is a cascade of reactions that can lead to acute heart malfunction and shock. It can be life-threatening if it is not treated quickly.

In most asthmatics, IgE levels are usually very high, and the immune response to allergens causes excessive mucus production and tightening of airways. This makes it extremely difficult to breathe, causing an asthma attack.

Such overreactions aside, the immune system is essential to our survival. For example, the immune system converts the vaccines we receive as children into lifetime protection from diseases.

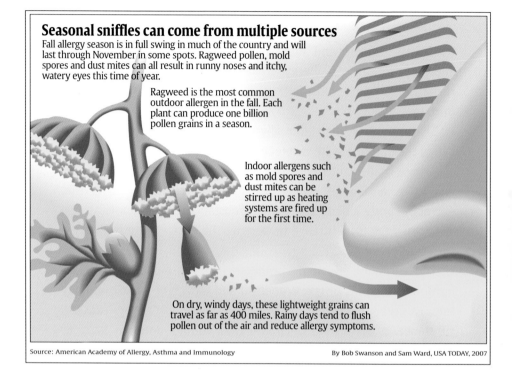

Seasonal sniffles can come from multiple sources

Fall allergy season is in full swing in much of the country and will last through November in some spots. Ragweed pollen, mold spores and dust mites can all result in runny noses and itchy, watery eyes this time of year.

Ragweed is the most common outdoor allergen in the fall. Each plant can produce one billion pollen grains in a season.

Indoor allergens such as mold spores and dust mites can be stirred up as heating systems are fired up for the first time.

On dry, windy days, these lightweight grains can travel as far as 400 miles. Rainy days tend to flush pollen out of the air and reduce allergy symptoms.

Source: American Academy of Allergy, Asthma and Immunology   By Bob Swanson and Sam Ward, USA TODAY, 2007

The immune system also keeps us from getting a bad infection every time we scrape a knee or cut a finger. Among people with asthma, more than 90 percent of children, 70 percent of young adults, and 50 percent of older adults have asthma attacks as a result of allergic reactions.

The list of known allergenic triggers is almost endless. But certain factors commonly turn up as triggers. Among the most common allergy-producing triggers are tiny airborne particles that easily float into the nose or mouth and down through the airways. These include microscopic particles from the animal kingdom. Feathers, wool and other animal fibers, pet hairs and dander, and particles of dead cockroaches can be found in the nooks and crannies of homes. Other triggers are the pollens and mold spores from living trees and plants—birch trees are particularly potent allergen producers—and in dried grasses such as hay. These plant allergens travel on the air only seasonally. However, they can be very troublesome when they are out and about.

Reactions can also be caused by chemical triggers in food and other substances people consume. For example, certain preservatives—such as the sulfites in hot dogs and the wax on store-bought apples—

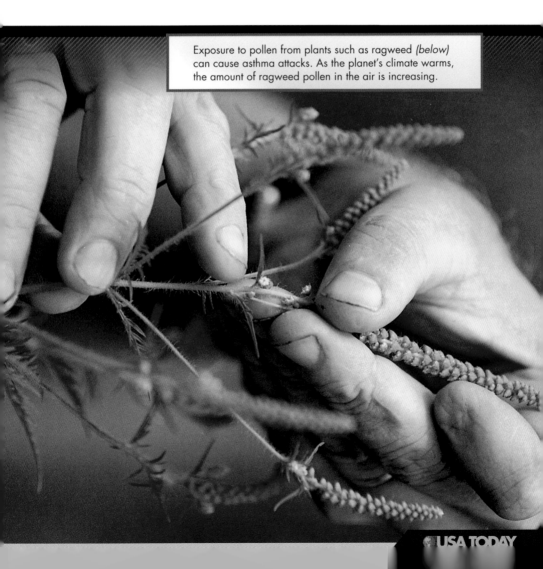

Exposure to pollen from plants such as ragweed *(below)* can cause asthma attacks. As the planet's climate warms, the amount of ragweed pollen in the air is increasing.

Eating certain foods—such as milk, eggs, soy, and wheat products *(all pictured above)*—can trigger asthma. For this reason, many asthmatics pay careful attention to their diets.

can bring on an asthma attack in some children. Food colorings are triggers for other asthmatics. Milk, eggs, soy, and wheat products are known contributors to asthma for many people. Aspirin, ibuprofen, and other common painkillers can set off an episode of wheezing and coughing in some people.

Some people with asthma may tolerate one substance by itself, but when the substance is combined with another, it is enough to cause a serious immune reaction. It's also possible for a person to be allergic to almost all of the triggers described.

www.usatoday.com

USA TODAY

Life

SECTION D

February 11, 2008

From the Pages of USA TODAY

Warm up to winter walks

Does a walk, run, or skate in the cold trigger your asthma symptoms? The key culprits are the dryness of winter air, combined with the sensation of cold on your face, says a report from the American College of Sports Medicine.

A solution for many: wear a scarf or balaclava [ski mask] over your lower face. That way, the air you breathe in will be slightly humidified, and your face will stay warmer.

—Kim Painter

Asthma triggers that are not, strictly speaking, allergy-based include:

- seasonal sinus infections, or more common respiratory infections, such as a cold or the flu
- vigorous exercise, including sports and play
- exposure to sudden temperature changes, such as moving out of the sun into an air-conditioned room or the other way around
- exposure to dry wind
- weather changes that disturb the environment, especially those that keep pollen and pollutants from being blown away
- electrical storms
- cigarette smoke, or smoke from wood fires or charcoal grills
- strong fumes or odors from items such as paint, gasoline, perfumes and scented soaps, household cleaners, and some cooking odors, especially those produced by frying foods

- strong emotions, including excitement, stress, sadness, or anxiety
- laughing or crying and their associated rapid breathing, which irritates the airways
- heartburn or indigestion caused by stomach acids rising into the throat and dripping down into the airways (known technically as gastroesophageal reflux or GERD)

About half of all young asthma sufferers can look forward to a big improvement in if not a total absence of asthma symptoms in their later teen years. The mature human body has larger airways, bringing greater ease of breathing. This growth probably explains why the ratio of boy to girl asthmatics changes in later adolescence. The boys, who once lagged behind girls in the growth curve, end up on average being larger, with bigger bronchial trees. But even when a person seems to outgrow asthma, the underlying tendency toward asthma still remains. It will always be possible for the symptoms to return under the right circumstances, such as a serious viral infection. Fortunately, with so much asthma information available, and with so many treatments developed to fit individual needs, most people are able to manage the symptoms of asthma.

The Trials of Teddy Roosevelt

Theodore (Teddy) Roosevelt (1858–1919) and his family spent much of his childhood coping uncomfortably with asthma. In the nineteenth century, when the future president was a boy, there were no medications to reduce airway inflammation (irritation and and swelling) and no satisfactory therapies to ease Teddy's discomfort. Each asthma attack was met with a sense that it could be life threatening—and it was. The Roosevelts were told that Teddy might do better with fresher air. When Teddy was eleven, the family set out on a tour of several European countries in search of relief for their son.

Teddy's mother administered home remedies that made him sick to his stomach. These remedies were based on the theory that ridding the body of food would disrupt the asthma. Teddy took nauseating mixtures of garlic, mustard seed, and squill (an herb), as well as whiskey and gin, opium mixed with wine, and chloroform. Though some children were given medicinal cigarettes of chopped camphor and jimson weed, Teddy's father had him smoke cigars. Some medical experts at that time recommended nicotine poisoning as a surefire way to stop the asthma attacks.

Teddy Roosevelt's health gradually improved as he grew into adulthood. He went on to become an outdoorsman, a big-game hunter, the hero on horseback of the Spanish-American War (1898), and twenty-sixth president of the United States (1901–1909). While he was never entirely free of asthma, it ceased to define his life sometime around his fifteenth birthday.

CHAPTER TWO

DIAGNOSIS: ASTHMA

Lara thought she was just like most other kids. In the springtime, she would sneeze a lot and have problems breathing when she went outside. But she noticed that a lot of people had the same symptoms when the weather was nice. Lara also noticed that she had the same symptoms after cuddling with her cat. She figured the cat had some dirt or dust in its fur, and it was normal to have a reaction to that.

But one afternoon she had so much trouble breathing that she started to panic. She sat still and quiet, and eventually her breathing went back to normal. Lara did not want to go to the doctor, so she didn't tell her parents about these episodes. But after she had two more scary episodes where she couldn't breathe, she knew she couldn't keep it a secret any longer.

Lara's parents brought her to the family doctor to be checked out. The doctor was calm and kind. She explained that Lara probably had allergy-induced asthma and that the next step would be to have some simple tests. The idea of having tests was scary at first. But once Lara realized that they would help her figure out what was wrong, she felt much better.

It may take a number of respiratory attacks before a person realizes that asthma is causing coughing and wheezing. That's because asthma looks like a number of other conditions. Some asthmatic children and young people are first diagnosed as having a chest infection, such as chronic bronchitis or walking pneumonia. Both of these diseases also involve the lungs, causing coughing and difficulty breathing. But these diseases generally go away after a few days or weeks, particularly after the patient takes a round of antibiotic medicines.

At some point, however, the asthmatic has a string of full-blown attacks. These are usually enough to differentiate asthma from other respiratory events. Often these attacks, or "flare-ups" as doctors often call them, begin at night. Severe coughing and breathlessness interrupt sleep, sometimes in an alarming way. The family doctor or pediatrician is usually the one to diagnose the condition. But if the symptoms seem severe or if they greatly differ from the usual symptoms, the doctor may suggest seeing a specialist. This is someone who has training and experience in a particular area of medicine.

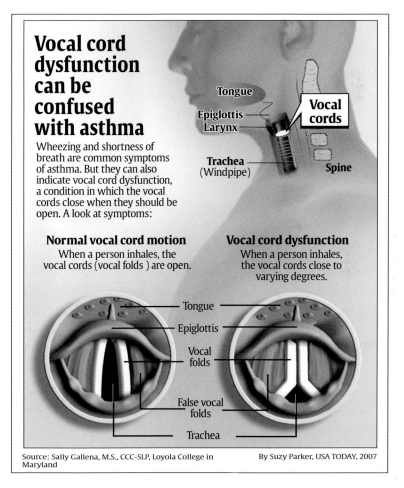

Vocal cord dysfunction can be confused with asthma

Wheezing and shortness of breath are common symptoms of asthma. But they can also indicate vocal cord dysfunction, a condition in which the vocal cords close when they should be open. A look at symptoms:

Tongue
Epiglottis
Larynx
Vocal cords
Trachea (Windpipe)
Spine

Normal vocal cord motion
When a person inhales, the vocal cords (vocal folds) are open.

Vocal cord dysfunction
When a person inhales, the vocal cords close to varying degrees.

Tongue
Epiglottis
Vocal folds
False vocal folds
Trachea

Source: Sally Gallena, M.S., CCC-SLP, Loyola College in Maryland

By Suzy Parker, USA TODAY, 2007

Two kinds of specialists deal with asthma—pulmonologists and allergists. For some severe asthmatics, both kinds of doctors are needed to control their asthmatic symptoms. Allergists are especially equipped to identify the possible allergens that may cause the asthma. Pulmonologists concern themselves with diseases and disorders of the lungs and airways. Most family doctors can suggest good specialists in their region. Contacting the local office of the American Lung Association or the state medical society may also be helpful.

PERSONAL HISTORY

The process of figuring out what's disrupting a person's health almost always starts with a full medical workup. This is the medical term for an investigation worthy of a top police detective. The workup to determine if asthma is the problem generally is made up of four parts: a medical history, a physical examination, some laboratory tests, and a series of allergy tests.

Taking a medical history is the doctor's way of learning about what has gone on in the person's life so far. The doctor knows that some of these events may have a bearing on the person's present health complaint. Taking a history can last half an hour or more. The doctor will want to know if parents or any close relatives have ever had asthma or other allergies. A patient may also need to find out if his or her mother had any problems while she was pregnant. Some complications during pregnancy can make a baby more likely to develop asthma.

The doctor will also ask if either or both of the patient's parents smoke tobacco. Mothers who smoke during pregnancy or while they are nursing put their babies at increased risk of hypersensitivity. This can lead to allergies and asthma in the child. Also, toddlers who live in a house with smokers and breathe secondhand smoke are more likely to develop asthma later. This is because the very young child's

www.usatoday.com

Life
SECTION D

March 16, 2009

From the Pages of USA TODAY

Getting Dad, Mom to quit

Children of smokers often beg their parents to quit. Now those children—many of them too young to speak for themselves—are getting an assist from their pediatricians.

Pediatricians aren't just asking smoking parents to quit. In a program launching statewide in Massachusetts this month, they are helping parents quit—by writing prescriptions for nicotine gum and other quitting aides and by referring them to telephone counselors for continuing support.

"Anytime you can get a parent to quit, it's a win-win situation," says Jonathan Winickoff, assistant professor of pediatrics at MassGeneral Hospital for Children.

Parents who quit live longer, on average, he says. They are less likely to smoke during future pregnancies. And their children are less likely to suffer sudden infant death syndrome, impaired lung development, middle-ear infections and severe asthma. Those kids also are less likely to become smokers, says Winickoff, founder of the stop-smoking program Clinical Effort Against Secondhand Smoke Exposure (CEASE). It is sponsored by the American Academy of Pediatrics.

A nationwide study is under way to see how many parents CEASE helps to quit. But an earlier study found 40% of smoking parents set a quit date when asked by their child's pediatrician, Winickoff says.

–Kim Painter

immune system is only partially developed and is more sensitive to outside irritants.

The doctor will also ask whether the patient has ever had a severe viral infection, and if so, whether any unusual symptoms developed in the weeks and months that followed. The doctor will want to know how much time is spent indoors versus playing outdoors, and if playing vigorous sports and games brings on a lot of coughing and wheezing.

Kids and Asthma

A study out in 2010 links a condition called chorioamnionitis — an inflammation of the fetal membranes from a bacterial infection — to childhood asthma in those born prematurely.

• About 12.5% of U.S. births are preterm. More than half of all preterm deliveries are thought to be associated with chorioamnionitis.

• In 2006, 9.9 million Americans younger than 18 had been diagnosed with asthma.

• Asthma is about 25 percent more common among Native American, Alaskan Native and African-American children than among white children.

— compiled by USA TODAY

Sources: Archives of Pediatric and Adolescent Medicine; Journal of Allergy and Clinical Immunology

The doctor will also ask about any reactions to particular foods. Because milk and milk products turn up often as allergenic foods, the doctor will ask whether the patient was fed breast milk or formula as an infant. He or she may also ask if any skin allergies associated with milk developed in the early months. (Research has shown that breast-fed babies tend to have a lower rate of allergies than bottle-fed babies. This is because the mother's own immune system gives an added measure of protection to infants.)

Other likely questions may cover when the patient's symptoms first appeared and whether the family has always lived in the same house and community or moved one or more times. Another useful clue can come from the patient's sleeping patterns. Does the patient sleep well at night, or is there a lot of coughing when lying down? Everyone's lungs function less well during sleep. Lying flat makes it harder for the lungs to move mucus along. This increases the possibility that the mucus would clog an asthmatic's narrow airways. And, by the nature of our internal clocks (a daily cycle known as the circadian rhythm), the lungs are the least efficient around 4:00 A.M. For children and young people with asthma, this drop in lung efficiency is even more pronounced. So any problem that may have gone unnoticed during waking hours is more likely to be noticed when the patient is lying still and asleep.

The physician will also want to know some very specific things about the house in which the person lives. Are there are a lot of rugs or carpets on the floor? What kind of fuel is used to heat the house? Are there any pets, and where do the pets spend most of their time?

THE PHYSICAL EXAM

The physical exam begins with familiar procedures, such as measuring your height and weight, listening to your lungs and heartbeat, and taking your pulse. Asthmatic lungs often sound different because the air moving in and out is whistling through so many tight spaces. The exam then moves on to procedures called pulmonary function tests. Pulmonary function tests measure how well the lungs take in air, how much they can hold, how well the lungs use the air they have, and how well they expel it. The specialist compares the results of several of these tests with test results from healthy children of the same size and age. This gives clues to the nature and extent of breathing difficulties. The testing procedures are safe and painless. If the patient has asthma, these tests will be performed every few months to chart the patient's progress.

The most important pulmonary function test is carried out with a spirometer. This is a small machine that records both the total amount of air a patient is able to exhale from the lungs at one time and the rate at which exhaling occurs. To get this information, the patient stands in front of the device, grasps a hose connected to it, takes in a quick breath and then, with mouth over the mouthpiece, forcibly exhales. The results register as a curve on a graph. At the beginning of the curve is the number known as the forced expiratory volume (FEV). The FEV is registered during the first second of exhaling. At the other end of the graph curve is the FVC, or forced vital capacity. The FVC is recorded several seconds later and represents the total air exhaled over the entire period of exhalation. The doctor then compares the earlier and later values. If the lungs are operating normally, 60 percent to 80 percent of the air will be exhaled in the first second. A patient whose airways are obstructed by asthma, on the other hand, will have a lower relative FEV, because the narrowed passages slow down the air.

For children and young people with mild to moderate asthma, the spirometry test may be the only breathing test the doctor needs to make a positive diagnosis. If the doctors suspects severe asthma, more sophisticated function tests may be added. For example, the doctor can check to see if the alveoli in the lungs are efficiently transferring oxygen into the blood and eliminating carbon dioxide. The patient is asked to breathe in a known quantity of air. Then, as he or she exhales, the air is measured. The volume of carbon dioxide detected becomes a measure of the lungs' air-exchange process.

One problem with tests like this is that the person being tested may have respiratory troubles only every now and then. As a result, breathing may be nearly normal during the visit to the doctor's office. If this is the case, the doctor may send the patient home with a handheld gauge called a peak flow meter. (Your peak flow is the maximum amount of air exhaled from your lungs.) Like the spirometer, the peak flow meter also tests the degree to which the airways are narrowed. However, the peak flow meter is small enough to carry around. The patient is instructed to do self-testing several times over the next few days, recording scores along with date and time of day. Patients who are eventually diagnosed with asthma become very familiar with this tool. It is the quickest and most practical way to know how well asthma medications are working at any given time and if an increase in medicine is needed to prevent an attack.

A medical professional helps a young girl use a spirometer, which measures the rate at which air is expelled from the lungs. The spirometer test can help doctors determine if a patient has asthma.

Other pulmonary function tests include an exercise test and a challenge test. In the exercise test, the patient works out for six minutes on a treadmill or on a stationary bicycle. The test gives the doctor insight into the particular stresses that exercise places on the patient's lungs. Before, during, and after the exercise, the patient uses a peak flow meter. Most people with asthma will show a considerable drop in peak flow within minutes of engaging in vigorous exercise.

The challenge test, which is used less often, involves measuring lung function before and after inhaling a mist of a chemical called methacholine. The test is repeated several times until the patient shows a measurable decrease in lung function. People who demonstrate little or no reaction to methacholine mist even at higher levels are probably not asthmatic. Among those who do show sensitivity, the level at which the reaction occurs is a fairly good gauge of how severe the asthma is. Those who react to very small amounts are the most sensitive.

LAB TESTS

The third part of the workup, the lab tests, consists of chest X-rays, a blood test, urinalysis, and sometimes a sputum test. A radiologist begins by taking two X-ray views of the chest, one front to back and the other side to side. If the asthma is mild, the chest X-rays will be normal. If the asthma is more severe, the radiologist will see some evidence of the lungs being underinflated. Other signs may also show up. This includes evidence of air being trapped in the space between the outside of the lungs and the rib cage. The alignment of the ribs may also be abnormal due to pressure in the wrong places. As the patient's asthma is treated and brought under control, these signs and symptoms will disappear.

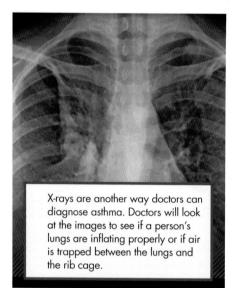

X-rays are another way doctors can diagnose asthma. Doctors will look at the images to see if a person's lungs are inflating properly or if air is trapped between the lungs and the rib cage.

The complete blood cell count (CBC) is taken by drawing a tiny amount of a patient's blood with a needle. The blood is then analyzed by a computer. It counts the numbers of red and white blood cells and looks for white cells carrying unusual numbers of antibodies. This could indicate an allergic response. Samples of urine, as well as of sputum (gooey stuff that comes up from deep in the chest when you cough) may also be examined.

The patient will probably be tested for specific allergic responses. This will most likely be done through a procedure known as skin testing. Typically with asthma patients, tiny amounts (less than 0.1 milliliter, or smaller than a drop) of a number of allergenic substances are used. They are scratched into the surface of the patient's skin, injected just below the top layer of skin, or applied to the skin on gauze patches. The location of each allergen is mapped

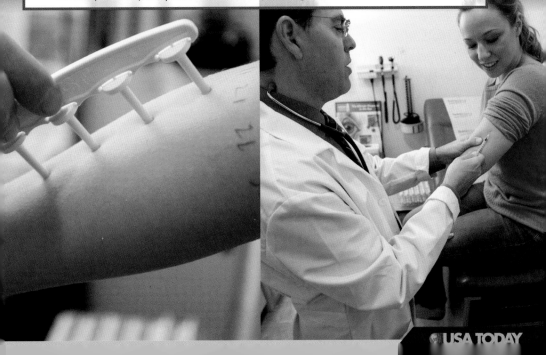

Allergic reactions can trigger asthma. To test for allergies, medical professionals perform tests that expose a person to different substances. The substances may be placed on the surface of the skin (below left) or injected below the skin (below right).

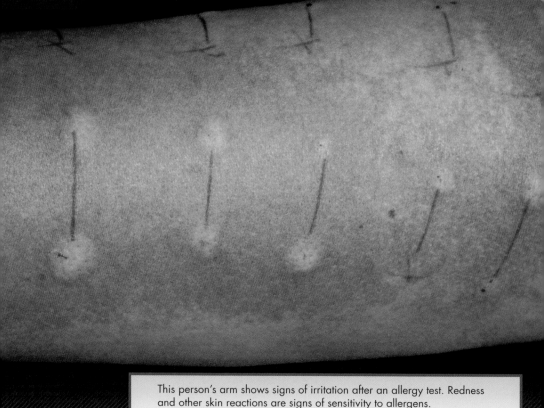

This person's arm shows signs of irritation after an allergy test. Redness and other skin reactions are signs of sensitivity to allergens.

and the skin is monitored for reactions at each location. Red, itchy spots may appear in as little as fifteen minutes, or they may take several hours. No matter the timing, skin reactions show an allergy to the test substance.

SCORING ASTHMA

Even before completing the tests with the patient, the doctor probably has a fairly good picture of the severity and type of asthma involved. This is important because the physician will apply this information to a set of guidelines developed by the U.S. government's National Asthma Education and Prevention Program. Doing this will help the doctor come up with the best possible treatment program for the individual. The guidelines represent current thinking in asthma management. According to the guidelines, most asthmatics fit into one of four broad categories: mild intermittent (off and on); mild persistent (ongoing); moderate persistent; and severe persistent.

People with mild intermittent asthma experience fewer than two wheezing episodes per week and fewer than two nighttime attacks per month. Their lung function is above 80 percent of what is considered normal for their age and size. Because they can interrupt their symptoms within minutes by taking a fast-acting medication, these people generally do not need to be on a daily regimen of medicines. Mild intermittent asthmatics may, in addition, have only a very limited number of substances that trigger their inflammation. They may go through whole seasons without any symptoms of asthma.

Children and young people who have slightly more than two wheezing episodes during the week and more than two nighttime attacks per month are described as having mild persistent asthma. Lung function tests show that their lungs still work at 80 percent of normal capacity. To maintain control of symptoms, they must take daily preventive medications. They may also use short-term drugs that open airways whenever they sense an attack coming on.

The third broad category of asthma is moderate persistent. People with moderate persistent asthma live with daily symptoms, frequent episodes of wheezing, and at least one nighttime flare-up per week. Their lung function is somewhere between 60 percent and 80 percent of normal. They need more medications to control their symptoms. But most manage to go about their lives in fairly routine ways otherwise.

A small minority of people falls into the category of having severe persistent asthma. They have continual symptoms and frequent attacks during the day and night. Until the asthma is properly diagnosed and under control, most of these asthmatics are able to live safely only by restricting their activities, taking large doses of medications, and making trips to the emergency room whenever an uncontrolled crisis occurs. Even after diagnosis, severe persistent asthmatics may need to restrict their activities. This is because their lung function tests show their breathing to be significantly weakened. They live with only 60 percent or less of normal lung function. Their medical regimens combine prevention and relief, but under stricter guidelines and using a greater range of drugs on a daily basis than those of people with less severe cases.

The four categories are broad, and every patient responds somewhat differently to treatment. Experienced doctors regard the four classifications only as a starting point for planning treatment. Sometimes, after patients are diagnosed, treated, and show improvement, their doctors may scale back treatment.

Categories of Asthma

TYPE OF ASTHMA	FREQUENCY OF SYMPTOMS	NORMAL LUNG FUNCTION	EFFECTIVE TREATMENT
mild intermittent	Fewer than two wheezing episodes per week; no more than two nighttime flare-ups each month	more than 80 percent	Fast-acting medication when needed
mild persistent	More than two wheezing episodes per week; more than two nighttime flare-ups each month	80 percent	Daily preventive medication; fast-acting medication when needed
moderate persistent	Daily symptoms; frequent wheezing; one or more nighttime flare-ups each week	60 to 80 percent	More and a larger variety of preventive medication; fast-acting medication when needed
severe persistent	Continual symptoms; frequent attacks occur night and day	60 percent or less	Restricted activity; large doses of a variety of daily medications

Based on guidelines from the National Asthma Education and Prevention Program

CHAPTER THREE

TAKING CONTROL

ophia is a sixteen-year-old girl with mild intermittent asthma. She is allergic to cats and some types of tree pollen. Once she discovered what caused her asthma attacks, she learned to limit her exposure to those triggers. She doesn't experience a lot of wheezing episodes— maybe one every couple of weeks. Because her asthma is not severe, her doctor only prescribed a fast-acting reliever medication. She uses this inhaler when her airways close up during an asthma attack.

Joey, her ten-year-old cousin, has severe persistent asthma. He has asthma flare-ups just about every day and night. Joey is sensitive to many allergens and has problems breathing during strenuous physical activity. He has to limit his activities, and he takes a lot of medication. Daily doses of a medicine called corticosteroids help to prevent his airways from swelling. Joey also has his reliever medication with him at all times. If a flare-up occurs, using his inhaler can save his life.

When you know how to control asthma, it no longer controls you. There are many different steps involved in managing asthma. These include understanding the course of treatment involved (medication and therapies), adjusting your environment as best you can, taking the proper precautions, and working together with doctors, teachers, coaches, friends, and family to manage your asthma.

MEDICATION

For many years, doctors believed that children with asthma needed medications only when they were in the middle of a full-blown asthma attack. The person would only take the medication when he or she was coughing, wheezing, and gasping for breath.

But by then, the sufferer's airways were already swollen, inflamed, and clogged with sticky mucus. With this approach, relief would come slowly at best. Sometimes it was necessary to go to the emergency room or even to spend a few days in the hospital to regain normal breathing patterns. These experiences can be very frightening and make an asthma patient even more anxious about his or her condition.

Doctors still advise some people with mild intermittent asthma attacks to take their medications "as needed" once their asthma is under routine control. These asthmatics gradually learn to recognize the signs of an asthma attack. They are able to use relief medications to ward off a full-blown flare-up.

But for most asthma patients with persistent to severe symptoms, the use of medications has changed dramatically. The goal is to get ahead of the disease by taking medications that prevent or greatly diminish the severity of asthma attacks long before they start. As doctors frequently explain to patients, when it comes to asthma

A doctor reviews medications with an asthma patient. Finding and working with a doctor you trust is a key part of managing asthma.

attacks, the longer one lasts, the worse it gets, and the worse it gets the longer it lasts. So, it's better to prevent it from getting started in the first place.

The cornerstone of prevention is to reduce the sensitivity of the airways. This kind of prevention has to be done on a daily basis, even when a patient is feeling good. Doctors prescribe two major classes of medications to manage asthma. These medications are grouped according to their primary usefulness in controlling asthma symptoms. Relievers are used for short-term relief. Controllers are medications for long-term management. Relievers and controllers are often used in combination. A doctor determines the exact combination of medications. He or she works on an ongoing basis to find the best possible program for each individual. What works today may be satisfactory for months or years. But it's more likely that the dosages will have to change as the seasons change, as allergic triggers shift, as the body grows older and larger, or even as the home environment changes. Anyone who gets to know asthma firsthand soon understands that no one treatment plan lasts forever.

All asthma medications include very powerful substances, so it's also important to use them in precisely the right doses and according to schedule. You might call it the Goldilocks

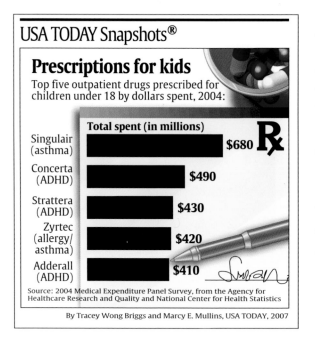

USA TODAY Snapshots®

Prescriptions for kids

Top five outpatient drugs prescribed for children under 18 by dollars spent, 2004:

Total spent (in millions)

Drug	Total spent (in millions)
Singulair (asthma)	$680
Concerta (ADHD)	$490
Strattera (ADHD)	$430
Zyrtec (allergy/asthma)	$420
Adderall (ADHD)	$410

Source: 2004 Medical Expenditure Panel Survey, from the Agency for Healthcare Research and Quality and National Center for Health Statistics

By Tracey Wong Briggs and Marcy E. Mullins, USA TODAY, 2007

Rule of Safe Medication: not too much, not too little, but just right. When children with asthma are young, their parents and their doctors manage their medications. But as they mature and are able to take more and more responsibility for themselves, it becomes each one's job—in consultation with a doctor—to keep track of what medicines to take and when. The best way to do this is to keep a daily diary.

RELIEVERS

Asthma relievers belong to a class of drugs called bronchodilators. Bronchodilators are used to relieve wheezing. In some cases, doctors prescribe them for use before or after exercise. The most effective bronchodilators are chemical messengers that seek out the smooth muscle cells around the airways (bronchi) and instruct them to relax (dilate). As the airways open wider, breathing

People with asthma learn to manage their medications on a daily basis. To avoid missing a dose or taking the wrong amount, many asthmatics keep daily journals *(above)* to track their medications.

quickly gets better. This may happen within five minutes of taking the medication. Bronchodilators stimulate certain nerve receptors in the body. Doctors and pharmacists call these particular stimulants beta-agonists or beta-adrenergics.

Many bronchodilator medications are delivered by metered-dose inhalers (MDIs). These are also known as puffers. Many inhalers are small devices that consist of a small canister of propellant gas (gas under pressure) screwed onto a small canister of liquid medicine. The user places the mouthpiece of the inhaler in the mouth, draws a breath inward, and at the same time presses the button that activates the device. A metered or measured amount of the reliever drug is propelled into the mouth and downward into the breathing passages.

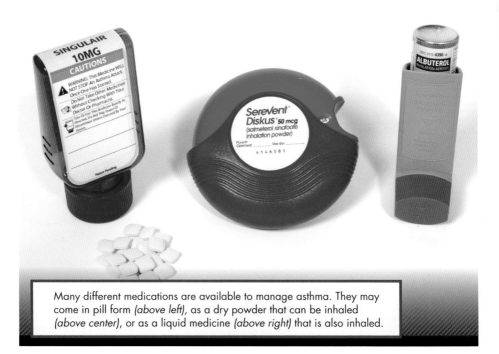

Many different medications are available to manage asthma. They may come in pill form *(above left)*, as a dry powder that can be inhaled *(above center)*, or as a liquid medicine *(above right)* that is also inhaled.

Bronchodilators are medicines that come in many forms, including inhalers, as shown above. These medicines open up constricted airways. They can also prevent asthma attacks triggered by exercise or cold air.

Some people have a hard time coordinating the instant of inhaling with pushing the button. As a result, the medication either shoots out into the room or never gets beyond the mouth , therefore failing to travel down the throat and into the bronchioles. To avoid this problem, an extra piece can be attached to the canister's mouthpiece. This spacer device is an extra chamber that traps the medicated mist until the user is ready to inhale deeply.

Other inhalers come in the form of a disk-shaped device filled with a liquid or dry powder medication. The disks do not use a propellant to force the medication out. Instead, the medication is delivered when the user inhales the metered dose from the mouthpiece.

www.usatoday.com

USA TODAY

Life

SECTION D

December 15, 2008

From the Pages of USA TODAY

Big changes for inhalers

The inhalers that millions of people use to treat asthma attacks are going green.

Old-style inhalers, which used ozone-destroying chlorofluorocarbons (CFCs), will not be sold in the USA after Dec. 31. In their place, doctors must prescribe and pharmacies must hand out new inhalers that use ozone-friendly propellants called hydrofluoroalkanes (HFAs).

The new drugs work at least as well as the old ones. And saving Earth's ozone layer certainly is a good thing, asthma experts say. There's just one problem: Lots of people with asthma have no idea the change is coming and are about to get new devices that work a little differently, need extra maintenance and cost more.

"It's one of the best-kept secrets," despite efforts by doctor and patient groups, says Ira Finegold, chief of allergy and clinical immunology at St. Luke's-Roosevelt Hospital in New York.

The new inhalers contain the drugs albuterol or levalbuterol, so-called bronchodilators. These drugs can quickly open airways during an asthma attack. People with some other breathing disorders use them, too. The change does not involve longer-acting inhaled drugs patients use every day to prevent symptoms. Four of those drugs are undergoing a safety review by the Food and Drug Administration.

Many patients already have the new inhalers. But prescription sales data indicate millions have not yet switched, says Nancy Sander, president of the Allergy & Asthma Network Mothers of Asthmatics in Fairfax, Va.

If calls to Sander's group are an indication, many people learn their inhalers are

People with asthma may find it hard to use an inhaler the first couple of times. Sometimes it takes a little while to get used to them. If you use an inhaler, be sure to ask your doctor or pharmacist to show you the right way to use the device. Otherwise, you may not be getting the correct dose to help relieve asthma symptoms.

People with asthma can also inhale relievers through a nebulizer.

changing when a pharmacist hands them one, along with a higher bill. "Many are confused," she says. "They go to the pharmacy to pick up their inhalers, and their $4 or $10 co-pay has gone to $30 or $35."

The reason for the price increase: The new inhalers, from four different manufacturers, are brand-name drugs; there is no generic version.

Sander says she has heard of family members sharing inhalers to cut costs. A better idea, she says, is to ask your doctor for a discount coupon or to see if the drug company can help. Allergy doctors, meanwhile, are lobbying insurers to lower co-pays.

Price isn't the only change. Some others:

- You have to clean them. Doctors always have told patients to clean their inhalers, but "nobody ever did it," says Dennis Spangler, chief medical officer at Atlanta [Georgia] Allergy & Asthma Clinic. With the old inhalers, that was OK; they still worked fine. The new inhalers will clog if not cleaned about once a week.

- You have to read the directions. Each of the new inhalers has slightly different requirements for priming, which involves spraying some doses into the air to make sure the device is ready. One brand must be discarded after six months. "All those people who open up the box and throw the insert away should read it, at least the first time," Finegold says.

- It's going to feel different. The new devices produce a softer, warmer spray. Many people fear the softer spray isn't working, but studies show more mist actually gets into airways, Finegold says.

The changeover is a great time for patients to assess how well they are controlling their asthma, the experts add.

Patients who use their inhalers frequently to stop symptoms such as shortness of breath, wheezing, coughing and chest tightness might need to do more to prevent attacks. Using additional drugs meant for daily use and eliminating allergy triggers can help.

—Kim Painter

This type of inhaler is larger and more expensive. It includes a special air pump and a close-fitting mouth mask or mouthpiece. The nebulizer delivers a continuous flow of medication. The medicine travels farther and faster than a regular inhaler can deliver, in a precisely measured dose. This makes it particularly effective in treating very young children who have a hard time

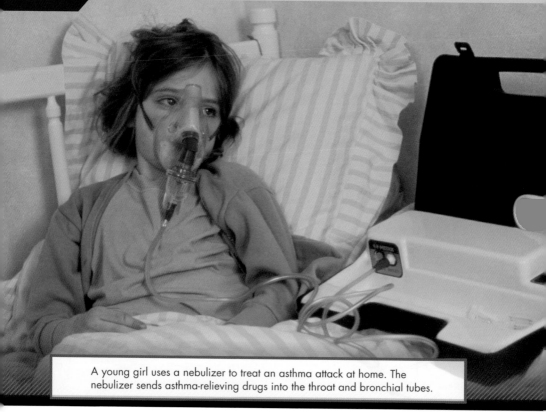

A young girl uses a nebulizer to treat an asthma attack at home. The nebulizer sends asthma-relieving drugs into the throat and bronchial tubes.

with other inhalers. The nebulizer is also favored in emergency treatments, when patients of any age may not be able to breathe in the medication on their own. Nebulizers are standard pieces of equipment in hospitals.

Bronchodilators do have some side effects. Medications that dilate the airways work like a hormone the body makes called epinephrine. This hormone is a chemical that can increase the heart rate, raise blood pressure, and cause nervousness and even tremors (shakes). If you notice any of these symptoms, you must tell your doctor. It may be necessary to change the dosage or type of medication.

Relief-bringing bronchodilators may also come as pills, tablets, and syrups. The effects of these oral medications are similar to the inhaled versions. However, because these systemic (affecting the whole body) medications need to be swallowed, digested, and circulated in the bloodstream before they can deliver relief, they work more slowly. Pills and syrups usually work too slowly for emergency situations, when speed is essential. But they are very good at delivering long-term relief. Systemic bronchodilators are also recommended as nighttime medicine following an attack, because they continue to work while you sleep.

CONTROLLERS

The other class of asthma drugs is controllers. They are the main part of daily management of chronic asthma. Most of them control the inflammation in the lining of the airways. This treatment is separate from controlling the tightness caused by sudden muscle contraction during an asthma attack.

Several classes of drugs qualify as controllers. The doctor's choice will depend upon the patient's age and the severity of the asthma. The most effective anti-inflammatory drugs belong to a class of substances known as hormones—specifically corticosteroids. The body naturally produces corticosteroids. These hormones circulate in the body all the time, carrying out a variety of important functions. One job is to control inflammation wherever it may occur.

However, the natural corticosteroids in people with moderate to severe persistent asthma cannot keep up with the inflammation. One way to help out is by adding synthetic (artificial) corticosteroids that mimic the effects of the natural ones. Controller corticosteroids may be inhaled or taken as pills. They work more slowly than the relievers. In many cases, a person with asthma must take them for weeks or months in order to gain the desired benefits. (Corticosteroids are not the steroids that some athletes use illegally and dangerously for body building. Asthma corticosteroids are safe and legal when used as prescribed.)

Individuals with mild persistent asthma may take a corticosteroid. It is more likely that they will be prescribed cromolyn sodium, another kind of anti-inflammatory controller. This somewhat milder drug is available in a couple of inhalant forms. It can take about four weeks of use for drugs in the cromolyn family to have a beneficial impact.

Another kind of controller is a class of drugs known as leukotriene pathway inhibitors (LPIs). LPIs interfere with the production of irritating substances in the airways. When these inhibitors go to work, less mucus and fewer histamines build up to irritate the cells lining the airways. They also seem to boost the activity of the other anti-inflammatory drugs, particularly the corticosteroids. This makes it possible to reduce the total dosage of all medications.

MEDICATING BY STEPS

Most physicians follow a series of step-by-step guidelines to prescribing medications. The National Institutes of Health (NIH), the U.S. agency that directs government health research, established these guidelines. For treating asthma and other conditions, the guidelines recommend starting at or above the level of treatment that matches the seriousness of current symptoms. Once normal or near-normal lung function is achieved, and the recurring attacks have been greatly reduced, a physician and patient can work on stepping down treatment.

In this model of treatment, the physician first determines the frequency and severity of the patient's asthma. This analysis yields a rating of severe persistent (step 4), moderate persistent (step 3), mild persistent (step 2), or intermittent (step 1). The physician then prescribes a plan for bringing the asthma under control quickly and aggressively. The plan, which should be in writing, includes prescribed medications and other recommendations. It spells out the precise amount of each medication and the time of day to take it. The patient is shown how to use the metered-dose inhaler. He or she will also learn to monitor breathing with a peak flow meter. Patients are asked to keep a daily diary, noting when the asthma was under control, when flare-ups occurred, and what kinds of events triggered the onset of asthmatic episodes. If specific allergens have been identified as triggers, the doctor and patient discuss ways to avoid them or minimize their impact. Emergency plans for how to handle a severe flare-up are also discussed.

In the first few days of treatment, some parts of the treatment plan may be confusing or uncomfortable for asthma patients. Patients may need to call their doctor or make additional visits to the doctor's office for clarification or additional assessment. About three months later, the doctor, patient, and family sit down to review how things are going. If the patient's asthma is under good control, the doctor may decide to step down the treatment to the next level to see how well the patient responds. The patient who arrived with symptoms in the severe persistent (step 4) category might—after several weeks of treatment—do fine at the moderate persistent (step 3) level. Some might even hope to have their therapy cut back in gradual stages to the level of mild persistent (step 2). Whatever the outcome, the patient continues to be monitored on a regular basis. The doctor tweaks the treatment plan until everyone is satisfied that the patient has reached a personal best.

FIGHTING ALLERGENS AND IRRITANTS

Effective medications have made a big difference in controlling asthma. Avoiding many of the situations that trigger asthma attacks is just as important. A person with allergy-based asthma must work hard to reduce specific types of exposure.

FOOD ALLERGIES

If a food allergy is causing asthma symptoms, the obvious thing is to avoid eating that food as much as possible. For many foods, that's fairly simple. But what about foods that are common ingredients in a lot of other foods, especially in prepared and packaged foods? When buying food, always check the ingredients list on food labels. Avoid eating new things unless you know you are not allergic to any of the ingredients. Your doctor may have some suggestions too, and you may be referred to a nutritionist, an expert in healthy eating. Together you can develop strategies for knowing what types of foods and food ingredients are off-limits.

If you are on a restricted diet, you must find out if you need to take vitamins or mineral supplements. This is especially true for people who have an allergy to milk and milk products. For some people, milk triggers the production of excess mucus, which can lead to

Nutrition Facts

Serving Size 2 whole crackers (27g)
Servings Per Container about 15

Amount Per Serving

Calories 110   Calories from Fat 10

	% Daily Value*
Total Fat 1g	**2%**
Saturated Fat 0g	**0%**
Trans Fat 0g	
Polyunsaturated Fat 0g	
Monounsaturated Fat 0g	
Cholesterol 0mg	**0%**
Sodium 130mg	**5%**
Total Carbohydrate 22g	**7%**
Dietary Fiber 1g	**4%**
Sugars 7g	
Protein 2g	

Iron 6%

Not a significant source of vitamin A, vitamin C, and calcium.

*Percent Daily Values are based on a 2,000 calorie diet. Your daily values may be higher or lower depending on your calorie needs:

		Calories:	2,000	2,500
Total Fat	Less than		65g	80g
Saturated Fat	Less than		20g	25g
Cholesterol	Less than		300mg	300mg
Sodium	Less than		2,400mg	2,400mg
Total Carbohydrate			300g	375g
Dietary Fiber			25g	30g

Calories per gram:
Fat 9   •   Carbohydrate 4   •   Protein 4

INGREDIENTS: ENRICHED **WHEAT** FLOUR (**WHEAT** FLOUR, NIACIN, REDUCED IRON, THIAMIN MONONITRATE, RIBOFLAVIN AND FOLIC ACID), GRAHAM FLOUR, SUGAR, HIGH FRUCTOSE CORN SYRUP, HONEY, CONTAINS TWO PERCENT OR LESS OF: VEGETABLE OIL (CONTAINS ONE OR MORE OF THE FOLLOWING OILS: INTERESTERIFIED **SOYBEAN**, CANOLA) WITH CITRIC ACID AND TBHQ ADDED TO PRESERVE FRESHNESS, MOLASSES, SODIUM BICARBONATE, SALT, **SOY** LECITHIN (AN EMULSIFIER), AMMONIUM BICARBONATE, MALTED CEREAL SYRUP, NATURAL AND ARTIFICIAL FLAVORS, SODIUM SULFITE AND ENZYMES.

Understanding what is in the food we eat is an important way to manage health.

more coughing. If you have to cut back on milk, be sure you take a calcium supplement. Calcium is a key nutrient throughout life, but it is absolutely necessary while the human body is growing. A doctor or nutritionist can advise a young person with asthma and his or her family how much calcium is needed.

Some people have an asthmatic response to aspirin or medications containing aspirin. For these asthmatics, the consequences of taking those medications can be severe. If you fall into this category, be sure to discuss with your doctor which over-the-counter drugs you should avoid. When in doubt, read the labels and ask a pharmacist or doctor. Alka-Seltzer, Advil, Motrin, and some cold and cough medications contain small amounts of aspirin that can cause an adverse reaction in some people with asthma.

ENVIRONMENTAL ALLERGENS

Many environmental allergens can stir up trouble for asthmatics at work, at school, or at home. It's hard to control work and school environments, but there are some steps that can be taken. People with severe allergies should tell their teachers, classmates, bosses, or coworkers. Together they can discuss how to prevent the asthmatic from having a flare-up as a result of allergens in the office or classroom.

Asthmatics have more control over the asthma triggers in their homes. The home should be made as allergen-free as possible. This is especially important for an asthmatic's bedroom. Pillows and other bedding made of feathers, goose down, or kapok often cause allergic reactions. Replace them with synthetic materials. Cotton blankets are usually better than wool. Zip mattresses, box springs, and pillows into plastic covers, to prevent allergens from collecting in the fabrics and coils of bedding. Wash sheets, pillowcases, and blankets every

Every house has millions of tiny dust mites *(microscopic view above)*, which live in carpets, bedding, and furniture. Dust mites can be a trigger for asthma.

week. This will help to remove most of the allergens. Stuffed toys may also make allergies worse. Children should avoid taking them to bed. Wash stuffed toys once a week in very hot water.

For years, experts believed that dust was a major asthma trigger. But the real problem is the little organisms that attach themselves to dust. These tiny dust mites can only be seen under a microscope. In a typical room, thousands of these crab-like mites live on dusty surfaces, carpets, rugs, curtains, and bedding. Research has shown that even if you vacuum a carpet for an hour each day for a whole year, you can't get rid of all of the dust mites.

One way to fight dust mites is to remove carpets, rugs, and unnecessary toys and games from the asthmatic person's bedroom. Put clothes away in closets or drawers. Dust and vacuum at least once or twice a week. Depending on the severity of the asthma, a family may need to take these dust-control measures to other rooms in the house.

Cockroaches are another hard-to-manage environmental allergen. Many asthmatics are allergic to the bugs' bodies, saliva, and feces (waste). These scurrying bugs can be found in many different types of homes. They are most often found in city apartments or in urban areas. In fact, the unusually high rate of asthma among inner-city children is largely due to cockroaches. These bugs tend to live in the walls of older buildings. Insect sprays and other extermination methods can control cockroach populations. An asthmatic should stay away while the home is being sprayed for cockroaches or other bugs. The bug-killing chemicals can also cause flare-ups.

Pollen is another common allergen. Pollen comes from trees, flowers, grasses, and other plants. Many people experience strong pollen allergies when certain plants are flowering or blooming. It is hard to avoid pollen completely, but people with asthma can reduce their exposure. To keep the pollen out of the home, keep windows

Oak pollen *(microscopic view below)* is one of many airborne pollen grains that may cause allergic reactions in humans.

www.usatoday.com

USA TODAY

Life

SECTION D

August 25, 2009

From the Pages of USA TODAY

Pollens are the enemy

Starting to sneeze? It's that season for folks allergic to ragweed, one of the most common causes of nasal allergy symptoms. Though medication can help, doctors say the best way to feel better is to limit exposure to irritating pollens.

Here are five tips:

- Keep house and car windows closed and use the air conditioner.
- Avoid outdoor activities before 10 A.M., when pollen levels are heaviest.
- Wear a mask to mow the lawn or work in the garden.
- Keep pollen off your pillow by showering before bed.
- Learn more from the American College of Allergy & Immunology at acaai.org/public/advice/rhin.htm.

—USA TODAY staff

closed. When it is hot, an air conditioner will cool the air while at the same time filtering out pollen and other allergens. Don't bring your shoes, jackets, or outdoor clothes into the bedroom. Showering and washing your hair when you've spent time outdoors will help get rid of pollen and other allergens. During warm times of the year, weather forecasts often include pollen counts. These counts tell you what kind and how much pollen is in the air. If possible, try to avoid spending a lot of time outside on days when the pollen count is high.

Humidity levels can also affect environmental allergens. A humid environment supports the growth of mold spores. Mold is a common allergen. A dehumidifier can help keep the house less humid. The dehumidifier should be cleaned periodically so that mold does not grow inside.

The family car can also have asthma triggers. When mold spores and pollen are in the air, keep the car windows closed. The car's air-conditioning filter should be cleaned regularly. Regular vacuuming of the car's upholstery and carpeting will also help.

PETS

Pets are one of the toughest problems for families dealing with asthma. Many kinds of pets have dander, or the animal form of dandruff. Animals naturally shed these tiny flakes of skin every day. Animal dander is a major allergen for many asthmatics. For that reason, cats, dogs, hamsters, and other furry pets can be unhealthy for people with asthma. Dust, dander, and feathers from birds can also trigger asthma flare-ups.

For many families, giving up a beloved family pet is a very difficult decision. Most people only consider that as a last resort. But there are some ways to deal with asthma in a home with pets. If possible, give pets a weekly bath. (Check with a vet or pet expert for advice on bathing pets.) People with asthma should not let their pets sleep on human beds,

Animal dander is a major asthma trigger. For that reason, people with asthma should not let pets with fur sleep on their beds. In fact, it's a good idea to keep furry and feathered pets out of bedrooms entirely, if at all possible.

couches, or chairs. In fact, you should try to keep the pets out of the bedroom at all times. Make sure to dust, vacuum, and generally clean the whole house on a regular basis.

For people with severe asthma, it may be too much to have furry or feathered pets in the house at all. Certain breeds, or types, of dogs and cats are supposedly hypoallergenic and do not cause allergic reactions. Some people have milder reactions to these breeds, but scientists haven't declared any dog or cat truly hypoallergenic. Fish, lizards, turtles, and other cold-blooded, furless pets are safe, dander-free alternatives.

Animals without hair or feathers, such as this boy's lizard, can be good alternative pets for people with asthma.

IMMUNOTHERAPY

Immunotherapy is another method for treating asthma. It is a technique that doctors use after asthma-triggering allergens have been identified. Immunotherapy involves injections of a purified solution of the known allergens. The objective of these shots is to force the immune system to become more familiar with the allergen. Over time, this may decrease the severity of the allergic reaction.

In the first phase of immunotherapy, the patient receives small amounts of allergens. The patient then gets slightly larger doses. At first, the injections are given once or twice a week. Eventually, the allergist may give the injections a few times a month, once a month, or even less frequently. The whole process of immunotherapy can take from three to five years. If the patient doesn't see major improvement in the first two years, immunotherapy is usually stopped.

ODORS AND AIRBORNE IRRITANTS

Not all substances that irritate airways are allergens. A number of other airborne irritants can trigger an asthma attack. Common irritants include smoke or odors from cigarettes or cigars, burning leaves, and grilling or frying foods. Fresh paint, glues, room deodorizers, oven cleaners, hair spray, lotions, and insect repellents can also be triggers. Other troublemakers are perfume, perfumed soaps, scented household products, and many cosmetics. Using unscented products may reduce asthma attacks.

If you have asthma and someone is spreading fertilizer on the lawn or using an insect spray, get as far away from the area as you can. Try to stay away for several hours, or until the chemical odors are weaker or gone. Watch out for scratch-and-sniff inserts in books and magazines. They can cause a flare-up when you least expect it.

www.usatoday.com

Life
SECTION D

March 22, 2010

| From the Pages of USA TODAY

Allergy shots get best results

The signs of spring are here. Trees are budding, grass is greening—and millions of allergy sufferers are taking pills, inhaling nasal sprays and avoiding the outdoors to control reactions that range from mild sniffles to dangerous asthma attacks.

Few, however, are using what may be the most effective treatment for uncontrolled symptoms: immunotherapy, or what most people know as allergy shots. The practice of injecting people with increasing amounts of the substances they are allergic to, so they can build gradual tolerance, is nearly 100 years old.

But U.S. surveys suggest shots are used by just 5% of nasal allergy patients.

"Inconvenience is the most likely reason," says Linda Cox, an allergist in Fort Lauderdale [Florida]. A typical treatment plan calls for a patient to come to a medical office once a week for several months, get a shot and wait 30 minutes (in case a rare, dangerous reaction occurs) and then continue less frequent shots for months or years more.

There's also a needle "fear factor," says Stanley Fineman, an Atlanta [Georgia] allergist and vice president of the American College of Allergy, Asthma & Immunology. And costs for the shots and office visits, which vary based on insurance coverage and other factors, may play a role.

But a recent study published in the *Annals of Allergy, Asthma and Immunology* showed children who get allergy shots had lower health care costs over 18 months than otherwise similar children. The cost of their shots, about $600, was more than made up by drug savings and

EXERCISE-INDUCED ASTHMA

For approximately 80 percent of people with asthma, exercise or an incident that leads to overexertion can be major triggers. Doctors call this exercise-induced asthma, or EIA. This reaction usually occurs either during or shortly after running, bike riding, participating in team sports, dancing, or some other lively physical activity. EIA fewer doctors' visits and hospitalizations, says Cox, who led the study. Immunotherapy also might help prevent asthma, a costly life-long condition.

So allergists are working to make the shots more appealing. Most efforts fall into two categories: non-shot alternatives and faster shot schedules.

Immunotherapy without shots is standard in Europe. There, most doctors prescribe "sublingual [under the tongue] immunotherapy." Patients get liquids or pills containing extracts of grass pollen, dust mites, ragweed or other allergens and put a bit under their tongues at home each day.

But none of these products has been approved by the U.S. Food and Drug Administration. Some U.S. physicians prescribe sublingual use of liquid extracts approved for injections—but that is an unproven practice. And some studies on sublingual products under development have failed to show they work better than placebos.

That is changing, though. In one new study, a daily sublingual grass pollen pill reduced symptoms and medication use 26% in children and teens, says Michael Blaiss, clinical professor of pediatrics and medicine at the University of Tennessee Health Science Center in Memphis. Blaiss, a consultant to the drug's maker, Merck, presented the data at a recent meeting of the American Academy of Allergy, Asthma & Immunology. A study in adults found similar results, he says.

The pills have not been compared with shots and might cost more. They are not available now.

What is increasingly available: faster shot schedules. In so-called rush immunotherapy, allergists give patients numerous shots over one to three days to quickly build tolerance so patients can soon start coming just once or twice a month. In the somewhat slower "cluster" technique, patients might come once or twice a week for a month and get two or three shots at each visit to get a faster start. These patients all get antihistamines, steroids or other drugs to prevent dangerous reactions. Cox says the cluster technique is more widely used and thought safer. But Fineman says he safely gives rush patients nine to 20 injections in a day.

–*Kim Painter*

may discourage people with asthma from participating in school and after-school activities. But if you have a proper treatment plan, and follow the plan carefully, you should be able to enjoy sports and other activities.

People with chronic asthma need exercise even more than people who do not have asthma. Some doctors believe that strengthening

the heart and lungs can help a person fight the damage that asthma can cause. Tips for exercising in a safe way include:

- Sudden exposure to cold air is a common trigger of EIA. Minimize this risk by adjusting your lungs to the temperature change more slowly.
- Don't make sudden changes in activity level. Take time before vigorous activities to warm up. Cool down slowly from vigorous exercise rather than stopping all of a sudden.
- Pay attention to weather conditions. EIA is more likely to occur on very dry days. High winds can also dry out your airways and lead to a flare-up, so try to avoid outdoor activity on windy days.
- If possible, exercise outdoors on days when pollen and mold-spore counts are not high.

Asthma can be triggered by sudden exposure to cold air. Wearing scarves and other protective garments can help warm the air we breathe and prevent or minimize asthma attacks.

- Exercising while you have a cold or hay fever (pollen allergies) may be too hard. Postpone vigorous activities until you have recovered.
- If cold winter air consistently triggers EIA, try breathing through your nose more and through your mouth less. And loosely cover your nose and mouth with a scarf or wear a special cold-weather mask sold in many stores.
- A very good exercise environment for many people with asthma is a heated swimming

Asthma can also be brought on by exercising. Swimming in a heated pool is one form of exercise that is less likely to trigger exercise-induced asthma (EIA).

pool. The warm air and water temperatures can prevent EIA. But watch out for pools with too much chlorine and other chemicals. These chemicals can further irritate your airways. Many places have pools that use saline, or saltwater, solutions instead of traditional chlorine and pool chemicals. These saltwater pools may be less irritating for asthmatics sensitive to chlorine.

- Do not engage in vigorous exercise when your asthma is not under firm control, as you could trigger a full-blown attack.
- Always have your bronchodilators or other emergency medication nearby.

Discuss your exercise and physical activity concerns with your doctor. He or she may prescribe a specific pretreatment inhalant that you can use fifteen minutes before you start your exercise. Be sure your gym teachers and coaches know that you have EIA.

www.usatoday.com

USA TODAY

Life

SECTION D

November 18, 2009

From the Pages of USA TODAY

H1N1, asthma a dire combo

The day before Halloween, T.J. had what his parents believed was a little asthma flare-up. By Halloween night, he felt lousy enough to cut trick-or-treating short.

A week later, the 9-year-old was straining to breathe in the emergency room at Cincinnati Children's Hospital Medical Center [in Ohio] because of complications from an H1N1 influenza infection.

"By Sunday, Nov. 8, his cough turned into a croupy bark, and he started running a fever. It got to 102.9°F [39°C]. I knew it had gotten to be more than we could handle at home," says his mother, Jennifer. She had suspected flu but wasn't sure. His school had had significant numbers of children out, but his classroom hadn't seemed to be hit hard, she says.

While H1N1's effects in a healthy child can range anywhere from mild congestion and sore throat to serious respiratory illness, and even death, the 7 million American kids who have asthma are at a higher risk for complications and death if they contract the novel flu virus, says Tom Skinner of the Centers for Disease Control and Prevention [the CDC, in Atlanta, Georgia]. "We're seeing underlying health problems, including asthma, in about two-thirds of the estimated 540 children who have died from H1N1 complications," he says.

But the CDC and pediatric asthma experts say there are steps you can take to prevent H1N1, or swine flu, as well as seasonal flu, and ways to treat it if an infection does occur. "In children with asthma, the key issue is anticipation rather than reacting," says Erwin Gelfand, chair of pediatrics at National Jewish Health in Denver [Colorado], a hospital that specializes in treating children with respiratory conditions. Gelfand says a parent can ensure two things: vaccination and making sure a child's asthma is in control.

The advice goes even for children who get asthma only intermittently, says Tyra

Bryant-Stephens, medical director of the Community Asthma Prevention Program at Children's Hospital of Philadelphia [Pennsylvania]. "Children who only get asthma during exercise, with a cold, or during allergy season can also have serious complications from flu," Bryant-Stephens says.

T.J.'s parents gave him what asthma experts call "maintenance medications" every day: an oral Zyrtec (cetirizine) for allergies and the inhaled corticosteroid Flovent (fluticasone), which reduces inflammation in the lungs. They knew he needed the H1N1 vaccine, says T.J.'s mom, but it hadn't become available in their area yet. Unlike T.J., many asthmatic children do not take medications as prescribed, sometimes because of cost or parental concerns about side effects, Gelfand says.

As for vaccines, the CDC recommends that children with breathing issues get the shot form of the vaccine—two doses spread out by a month in those under age 9—instead of the nasal mist.

If a child does get flulike symptoms, there are steps caregivers should take, says Carolyn Kercsmar, director of the Asthma Center at Cincinnati Children's. She says if a child develops a fever, is feeling poorly, has chest pain, a bad cough or extreme fatigue, see a doctor right away.

T.J.'s parents took the correct steps, Kercsmar says. After additional home albuterol treatments didn't budge his symptoms, they scooted fast to the pediatrician, who sent him on to the ER. There, Jennifer says, "they did three back-to-back albuterol treatments—continuous for about an hour. He was so sick by then, poor thing."

He then received a cornucopia of drugs: Motrin to help reduce fever, antibiotics for atypical pneumonia that a chest X-ray revealed, and an intravenous line of magnesium sulfate to help further open up his airways. They dosed him with the steroid prednisone to simmer down inflammation, and he received pure oxygen through a nose mask, Jennifer says.

After an H1N1 swab came up positive, he was given Tamiflu (oseltamivir). "These are the children who can benefit from starting Tamiflu right away. It can turn a very nasty disease into one that's tolerable," says Kercsmar, who adds that it works best started within 48 hours, but even within 72 hours can help.

Jennifer reports that though her son's night in the hospital was rough, the turnaround was fast. "By noon the next day, T.J. was feeling well enough to eat a chili dog and a pretzel with cheese," she says. He went home that night.

–Mary Brophy Marcus

RESPIRATORY INFECTIONS

People with asthma should make an extra effort to avoid colds, flu, and other respiratory infections. One particularly important action you can take is to get a flu shot every year in the fall. Flu immunity lasts only a few months. But by getting one before the flu season begins, you have a high probability of getting through the winter months without a major respiratory infection. Try to stay away from people who have a cold or the flu. Washing your hands regularly and not touching your face can also keep the germs away.

People with asthma may require separate but aggressive treatment for sinus conditions. These problems often accompany and worsen asthma. The sinuses are the bony pockets behind the face and forehead in the skull. The lining of the sinuses may become

Children with asthma are at greater risk of complications if they get the flu. Getting a flu shot every year, like this child below, is one way to maintain good respiratory health.

inflamed when the sinuses have a lot of mucus. Treating the sinus conditions and the postnasal drip that accompanies them reduces cough and throat irritation. Doctors recommend nasal sprays, nasal irrigation, and antibiotics to clear up persistent infections.

Sinus problems and asthma tend to be most troublesome when a person is lying down. Some asthmatics have found that it helps to lie down with their head higher than the rest of the body. They do this by using a wedge-shaped pillow or extra pillows. The change in position helps drain mucus that can accumulate in the sinuses and airways.

Maintaining overall health can also help fight asthma. Getting enough sleep and eating the right foods helps to keep the body energized and healthy. If you have questions about proper sleep and nutrition, ask your doctor for help.

CHAPTER FOUR

LIVING WITH ASTHMA

Jaden was first diagnosed with asthma when he was five years old. Because he was so young at the time of his diagnosis, his parents managed his medication schedule and helped him prevent asthma attacks. As he got older and started going to school, Jaden learned more about taking care of his asthma on his own. His parents still played an active part in his asthma treatment, but Jaden made sure that he always had his emergency relief medication and monitored his activities.

Jaden was comfortable telling his teachers, coaches, and friends at school about his asthma. They helped keep an eye on him in case he was pushing himself too hard. They would also remind him to take a break if he started to wheeze. Though he was taking control of his health, Jaden knew that he didn't have to do it all on his own.

The most important part of living with asthma is taking care of yourself. You must take responsibility for knowing as much as you can about your condition. Get involved in your health! Ask questions and become familiar with the details of your care. Become skilled at reading your changing symptoms. This will make it easier to deal with flare-ups. And working together with the people in your life can help make the process easier.

TEAMING UP

The basic support team for a child or young person with asthma includes parents and doctors. It also includes those people and organizations who are knowledgeable about asthma and who are helpful and caring.

THE MEDICAL TEAM

The person with asthma may work with one or more specialists in allergies, immunology, and respiratory diseases. If he or she has severe asthma, it's likely that the relationships will continue over years of regular visits. The doctors monitor the effectiveness of treatment, repeat various diagnostic tests, and try out new drugs as needed. If the condition is mild to moderate and without complications, most young people with asthma can work with their pediatricians or family doctors.

Families work closely with medical professionals to manage asthma. Liking and trusting your medical team is key to managing your health, so make sure you find a doctor and clinic that you can work with long-term.

It's very important that patient and parents like and trust their doctor or team of doctors. Good medical care, like launching a space satellite or playing on a winning sports team, depends on teamwork. The patient should feel comfortable talking to his or her doctors. Everyone has to be willing to work hard at following the treatment plans the doctors propose. Doctors rely on their patients to notice the little things and to report what goes on when the doctor is not around. Only in those ways can a person with asthma get medical treatment that will help.

THE FAMILY

The patient's family is another important part of the team. The environment in which the person with asthma lives is important. Everyone who lives together must work to make the home environment a healthy place to live. This may mean sharing household duties, such as more frequent or thorough cleaning of the home. To help the person with asthma, family members may also have to change other habits, such as smoking or keeping certain types of pets.

Parents and siblings are important and helpful members of the asthma team. They can help monitor symptoms, administer drugs, drive to appointments, and communicate with doctors and teachers. They can also help the person with asthma manage stress and fear. As the person with asthma gets older, he or she may be less inclined to take parental advice or to share personal thoughts with parents. But parents are key players in the team and can be vital to making sure everything works smoothly to manage the person's asthma.

TEACHERS AND COACHES

A number of people at school should also be on the asthma "dream team." At the start of each school year, the parents of a young person with asthma will want to meet with teachers, coaches, and the school nurse. They can review what the young person's medical needs are. For many, this may mean nothing more than being excused from the classroom for a few minutes each day to take medication at the nurse's office. Coaches also need to understand the asthmatic person's needs, particularly since asthmatic attacks can erupt during

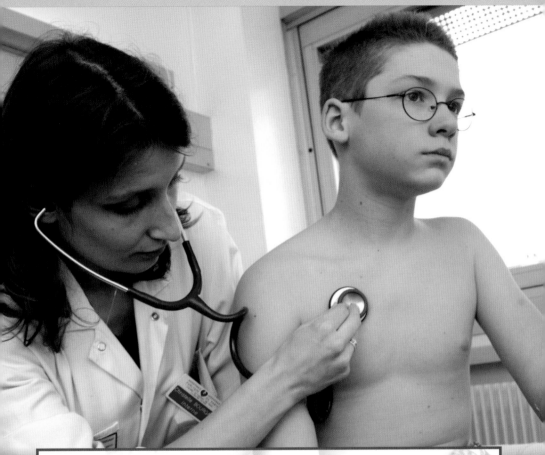

It's a good idea to share a child's asthma treatment plan with the school nurse. If a young person has an asthma attack while at school, the plan gives the nurse specific information about that individual to better manage the situation.

or immediately after strenuous exercise. The asthmatic's classroom may contain known allergenic triggers, such as a classroom pet. Parents may want to arrange to have their child transferred to a classroom without triggers such as these.

A full-blown asthma emergency may occur during school hours. It is critical that all those in a responsible position at school know what to do and whom to call. If possible, a copy of the student's asthma treatment plan should be on file in the nurse's office, along with the phone number of the treating physician and one or both parents.

www.usatoday.com

News
SECTION A

April 28, 2009

From the Pages of USA TODAY

Letter to the Editor: Help students with allergies at school

Living with food allergies can be a parent's nightmare. Currently, there is no prevention; immediate access to lifesaving medication can be the difference between life and death. For students whose schools insist on keeping all medications locked up in the clinic, this is a critical problem.

Allergy & Asthma Network Mothers of Asthmatics (AANMA) and its volunteers are changing this. Thanks to its advocacy work, Congress passed the 2004 Asthmatic Schoolchildren's Treatment and Health Management Act, which provided incentives for states to protect students' right to carry and self-administer their lifesaving asthma inhalers and anaphylaxis-fighting auto-injectable epinephrine.

Today, 41 states protect the rights of students who use auto-injectable epinephrine; 47 states have laws in place protecting the rights of students to carry their asthma inhalers.

Minutes count when anaphylaxis strikes. AANMA calls upon all states to protect students' right to carry lifesaving medication. After all, they only want to breathe.

—*Sandra J. Fusco-Walker*
Allergy & Asthma Network
Mothers of Asthmatics
Butler, N.J.

FRIENDS

Young people with asthma need the understanding and support of their friends. People with asthma often feel embarrassed about being different from their peers. They want to be just like everyone else, even in matters of health. A thoughtless comment or a silly joke can cause a young person with asthma to neglect his or her own care. This can lead to serious consequences.

Don't be afraid to tell friends and classmates about your asthma. Some may be curious about your inhaler. Tell them what it is for and how it helps you keep your asthma under control. It is important to let your friends know that there may be some restrictions on the things you can do. Friends can help you take it easy when you feel an asthma attack coming, or help you get to an adult when care is needed. But this doesn't mean that you should be treated differently. Everyone is entitled to be treated as an individual, not a condition. If you have a friend who has asthma, remember that support, understanding, and a positive approach are best for everyone concerned.

The support and understanding of friends is important to managing asthma and other health issues. Friends can get help for the asthmatic person if necessary and can be good listeners and problem solvers.

YOUR PEAK FLOW METER

When dealing with asthma, peak flow meter readings are very important. This is especially true for people with moderate to severe asthma. There are four types and two sizes of meters. The types are similar in basic design, but the size is important. Low-range meters are for young children. Standard-range meters are for older children and adults. Some peak flow meters are available over the counter, others only by prescription. Your doctor will tell you which model is best for you.

Individuals with asthma take an active role in managing their health. For example, this young woman is using a peak flow meter to monitor her lung function.

The peak flow meter measures the maximum speed that air can be forced out of the lungs. The meter measures lung function on a linear scale, just as rulers measure inches or centimeters. Readings that register below normal lung function indicate that the bronchial tubes are partially blocked. This is an early warning sign. Seeing these results gives you and your doctors a chance to adjust medications before an attack. A series of good readings on the meter can help your doctor step down your level of treatment. People with mild asthma are less likely to need a peak flow meter on a regular basis. But many still have one to take monthly readings.

The peak flow meter usually combines a numbered gauge with a three-color guide. Readings in the green represent normal to near-normal (100 percent to 80 percent) lung function. Readings in the yellow zone tell you that your lungs are operating at 80 percent to 50 percent of normal. The red zone at the bottom indicates lung function under 50 percent of normal. Everyone has his or her own personal high, medium, and low zones. Those numbers are based on tests performed periodically in the doctor's office. The doctor can help you set the adjustable color guide on your peak flow meter so that your readings are accurate for your condition.

When discussing the setting with your doctor, also find out how you and your parents need to respond to each reading. Generally speaking, a reading in the green zone means "keep doing what you're doing." A yellow zone reading indicates that you should take additional medications and perhaps postpone some activities until your lung function improves. A reading in the upper limits of the red zone suggests an immediate call to your doctor. A reading deep into the red is a signal that it's time for a trip to the emergency room. People with severe asthma rarely get to that level. This is because they use their peak flow meter regularly and follow their doctors' instructions.

Using a peak flow meter takes six steps:

1. Examine the sliding marker or arrow on the front of the meter. Be sure it's down at the bottom of the numbered gauge as you begin. Attach the removable mouthpiece.
2. Stand up. If you have any food or chewing gum in your mouth, take it out. Hold the peak flow meter horizontally, keeping your fingers free of the sliding marker.

3. Breathe in as deeply as you can. Seal your lips around the mouthpiece. (Keep your tongue out of the way too.) Blow out through the mouthpiece as hard and fast as you can. Stop when you can't blow anymore.
4. Write down the result.
5. Return the gauge to zero, and repeat steps 2, 3, and 4 twice more.
6. Choose your best attempt—the highest of the three readings. (One of your readings may be very different from the others. It probably indicates that you weren't trying hard enough and need to repeat the process once more.) Compare the best reading with your normal peak flow rate. If you are unsure about your normal number, ask your doctor.

Take readings on your peak flow meter at least two times a day, at the same times each day. A good time to make your first daily reading is right after you get out of bed in the morning. Most people with asthma find this to be their worst time of the day. An accurate morning reading gives you a very good indication of where you are. Take your second reading in early evening, maybe right after dinner. Be sure to write the numbers down.

THE DAILY DIARY

People with persistent asthma find that a daily diary is the best way to keep track of their peak flow meter readings. In fact, even people with asthma who are not using a peak flow meter can benefit from a daily diary. The diary can be as informal as a weekly wall calendar or a pocket notebook. It is a convenient way to track subtle changes in symptoms. You and your doctor can see if your asthma is improving or worsening. It helps the patient and doctor learn more about how to best control symptoms on a long-term basis.

A patient can record the times when one or another asthma symptom occurred. These may include coughing, wheezing, tightness in the chest, shortness of breath, inability to do normal activities, missed school, or nighttime awakening. The diary might also include any encounters with and reactions to known allergens.

You can use your diary to help you keep track of your daily medications. You might include the number of times in the morning and evening that you take each of your prescribed medications. You want to be sure to take the prescribed amount every day, on time. Taking either too little or too much of your various medicines can spell trouble.

Be sure to take the diary with you whenever you have a doctor's appointment. Your doctor may want to modify the treatment plan.

USING THE INHALER

Keep your bronchodilator inhaler handy at all times. When you go out, carry it with you. Check the canister often (or ask your parents to help you check) so that you know that it isn't almost empty. Be sure to have a replacement before you run out of medication. You can get a pretty good idea of how many days your supply will last by doing a little math. Look on the manufacturer's label to find the total number of puffs contained in an unopened puffer. Divide this by the average number of puffs you take per day to find the total days' supply. For example, if your puffer contains 200 puffs, and you ordinarily take 4 puffs in the morning and 4 at night, divide 200 by 8 to get 25 days. Count out 25 days on your calendar, and you will have a pretty good idea of when your current supply will run out. Mark

Using an inhaler can sometimes be tricky. For a person with asthma, it's important to make sure you know how to use yours. If you have questions or don't feel confident about using your inhaler, make sure to ask for help.

the date on the bottle for easy reference. At least a week before the end date, make sure you have a replacement.

Be just as careful about monitoring your supply of other medications. Don't rely only on your parents to know and take care of it. If you have any doubts about how to use your inhaler, ask your doctor or nurse for help. A study of asthma-inhalant users has shown that half of patients used the device incorrectly. This means that millions of people who think they are getting medication are not receiving the full dose of the drugs they need.

Let your doctor know if wheezing symptoms continue shortly after using the inhaler. Do not increase the dosage on your own. Do not be tempted to use the inhaler more often than prescribed. Bronchodilators are a powerful medicine. Your heart can be affected if you misuse them.

April 27, 2005

From the Pages of USA TODAY

Steelers' Bettis carries message to keep asthma under control

Asthma never stopped Jerome Bettis from becoming one of the NFL's top running backs, but the medical condition that attacks the respiratory system is always a threat to slow down the Pittsburgh Steelers star known as "The Bus."

That's why Bettis, 33, who has climbed to fifth on the NFL's all- time rushing list with 13,294 yards in 12 NFL seasons, is spreading an important message.

"A lot of times, asthmatics don't understand control," Bettis says. "They may think their condition is not that bad. But asthma is so unpredictable. . . . I'm urging people with asthma to confer with their doctors to get a game plan."

Bettis, chosen 10th in the 1993 NFL draft out of Notre Dame [a university in Indiana], says his most serious battle with asthma on the field occurred on a humid day in on Sept. 22, 1997. The inhaler he used on the sideline did little to alleviate continuous labored breathing.

"It felt like somebody put a plastic bag over my head," he recalls.

The "life-threatening" incident, he says, prompted him to become more aggressive in treating the condition, which involved medication.

"That was the key," Bettis says. "You

People with asthma lead active, satisfying lives. For example, retired NFL halfback Jerome Bettis *(above)* has asthma. During his NFL career, he was known for his power and for skillful footwork on the field.

pay more attention to it. And now if I'm tired or dizzy, I slow down. I won't try to do some of the things for as long if I have shortness of breath. The goal of all of this is for people with asthma not to be afraid to take a deep breath."

—*Jarrett Bell*

BREATHING EXERCISES

Learn how to do deep breathing and practice the technique regularly. Deep breathing helps to keep lungs clear and increases air supply. It is a critical exercise for normal lung growth. It's also a good way to take control over your situation when you feel an asthma attack coming on.

Long, slow, deep breaths give your diaphragm a good workout. When you exhale, the diaphragm pushes against your lungs, helping push the air out. The diaphragm lowers during inhalations. This creates a kind of vacuum that helps to pull additional air into the lungs as they increase in size. If you don't exercise your diaphragm, you may get as little as half the force (and half the oxygen) that a healthy, well-developed diaphragm is capable of providing. Many professional singers and athletes swear by the exercises too.

Here's how to exercise your diaphragm and your lungs:

- First, lie face-up on the floor with your back flat and a pillow placed under your knees. Put one hand on the upper part of your chest and the other hand on your stomach. Relax.
- Next, close your mouth and breathe in through your nose. Imagine that you are pushing the air deep down toward your stomach. Watch your hands. If you are deep breathing correctly, the hand on your chest will not move, but the hand on your stomach will rise slightly.
- Now, pretend that you have a straw between your lips. Forcefully blow out a tiny amount of air. Pause. Repeat again. You'll know you are doing it right if the exhaled air makes a little hissing sound as it slides out and your stomach stays still.
- Continue the exercise until it's easy and effortless. Then sit up and do the same thing. Then stand and repeat again. All these routines help to build strength in your diaphragm. It will give you greater breathing control and efficiency in all kinds of situations.

PLAYING DETECTIVE

Even if you and your doctor have identified the triggers of your asthma, don't assume that there's nothing more to discover. Other allergenic substances or circumstances may be lurking in the background. Your daily diary may help you pick up important clues that you and your doctor will find useful. Be sure you do your part by paying attention and keeping good records.

Every time you experience an attack or even a near-attack, try to think back over what happened right before. Do the events match your previous experiences? Were you exposed to the same kinds of allergenic substances? Is there something new? Are you doing something different that may explain a new and unexpected attack? Learn how your body feels when an attack is in the making. That way you can help yourself right away.

EMERGENCY PLANNING

Whatever you do, don't try to tough out an attack or pretend it isn't happening. If you feel that your airways are closing down, or that any of the other usual symptoms are developing, check it out with your peak flow meter. Follow the suggestions in your treatment plan accordingly.

Have an emergency plan in place for those rare occasions when you may need immediate attention. Your doctor will help you develop one. Be sure you and everyone else in your household knows how to carry out the plan. Pick an obvious location, such as the refrigerator door, and post the phone numbers of your health care professionals. Rehearse your emergency plan with your family until everyone is comfortable with it and knows what to do. Also prepare a medical information card with these same details. Include the name of the closest relative to contact in an emergency. Put the card in your wallet or bag. Carry it with you when you are away from home.

Asthma Action Plan

For: _____ Doctor: _____ Date: _____

Doctor's Phone Number _____ Hospital/Emergency Department Phone Number _____

GREEN ZONE

Doing Well

- No cough, wheeze, chest tightness, or shortness of breath during the day or night
- Can do usual activities

And, if a peak flow meter is used,

Peak flow: more than _____
(80 percent or more of my best peak flow)

My best peak flow is: _____

Take these long-term-control medicines each day (include an anti-inflammatory).

Medicine	How much to take	When to take it

Before exercise ❏ _____ ❏ 2 or ❏ 4 puffs 5 to 60 minutes before exercise

YELLOW ZONE

Asthma Is Getting Worse

- Cough, wheeze, chest tightness, or shortness of breath, or
- Waking at night due to asthma, or
- Can do some, but not all, usual activities

-Or-

Peak flow: _____ to _____
(50 to 79 percent of my best peak flow)

First Add: quick-relief medicine—and keep taking your GREEN ZONE medicine.

_____ ❏ 2 or ❏ 4 puffs, every 20 minutes for up to 1 hour
(short-acting beta₂-agonist) ❏ Nebulizer, once

Second If your symptoms (and peak flow, if used) return to GREEN ZONE after 1 hour of above treatment:

❏ Continue monitoring to be sure you stay in the green zone.

-Or-

If your symptoms (and peak flow, if used) do not return to GREEN ZONE after 1 hour of above treatment:

❏ Take: _____ ❏ 2 or ❏ 4 puffs or ❏ Nebulizer
(short-acting beta₂-agonist)

❏ Add: _____ mg per day. For _____ (3–10) days
(oral steroid)

❏ Call the doctor ❏ before / ❏ within _____ hours after taking the oral steroid.

RED ZONE

Medical Alert!

- Very short of breath, or
- Quick-relief medicines have not helped, or
- Cannot do usual activities, or
- Symptoms are same or get worse after 24 hours in Yellow Zone

-Or-

Peak flow: less than _____
(50 percent of my best peak flow)

Take this medicine:

❏ _____ ❏ 4 or ❏ 6 puffs or ❏ Nebulizer
(short-acting beta₂-agonist)

❏ _____ mg
(oral steroid)

Then call your doctor NOW. Go to the hospital or call an ambulance if:

- You are still in the red zone after 15 minutes AND
- You have not reached your doctor.

DANGER SIGNS

- Trouble walking and talking due to shortness of breath
- Lips or fingernails are blue

- Take ❏ 4 or ❏ 6 puffs of your quick-relief medicine AND
- Go to the hospital or call for an ambulance _____ NOW!
(phone)

An asthma action plan can help a person with asthma gather and track information about his or her medications and doctors. Additionally, it can help friends, family, and others know what to do in case of an emergency.

Many people also wear a medical-alert bracelet or something similar. In emergencies, it provides information about your condition and whom to contact in an emergency. If you're gasping for breath, you might not be able to explain what is going on. With medical identification, you will be able to point to the card or bracelet. Medical emergency staff and many other people know to look for these bracelets. Then you can focus on taking the deep breaths your body needs until help arrives.

Many people with chronic health conditions wear medical alert bracelets in case of emergency. They are an inexpensive and effective way to share critical information about your health no matter where you are.

CHAPTER FIVE

HEALTHY MIND, HEALTHY BODY

For years Leila struggled with her severe persistent asthma. She took daily preventive medications, used her inhaler frequently, and had to limit her physical activities. When she was younger—before her asthma worsened—she loved to play soccer and softball. But as a teenager, she wasn't able to join her high school's sports teams. Leila was very angry and often fought with her parents, her friends, and even her doctors. She felt like her asthma was keeping her from doing anything fun or interesting. Leila eventually stopped going out with friends and wanted to stay in bed. She cried all the time.

Fortunately, Leila's parents brought her to a psychotherapist. The psychotherapist sat with Leila and encouraged her to talk about what was bothering her. Leila didn't want to talk to her at first, but eventually she opened up about how she felt alone and helpless because of her asthma. After many sessions, the psychotherapist helped Leila to understand that she wasn't alone—her parents, friends, and teachers wanted to help. She helped Leila to understand that there were other things that she was good at besides sports.

Leila also joined a support group made up other teens with asthma and serious diseases. Together, they talked about their feelings and what they could do to feel better. Leila still gets angry every now and then, but she knows that she's not alone and that talking about her problems does help.

Any health condition that makes a person feel different physically is likely to have emotional consequences. It can affect self-esteem and feelings about the future. As a result, some people don't follow their everyday asthma treatment plan. This turns what could be a manageable health problem into a big or life-threatening problem.

Asthma is a real disease. In years past, experts thought that people made up asthma symptoms to get attention. They also believed that only people who worried too much had these symptoms. But asthma is a true physical condition of the airways and the lungs. It actually starts in the individual cells that make up the respiratory sys-

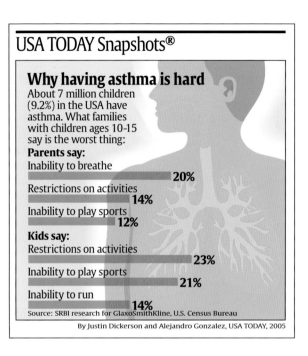

USA TODAY Snapshots®

Why having asthma is hard

About 7 million children (9.2%) in the USA have asthma. What families with children ages 10-15 say is the worst thing:

Parents say:
Inability to breathe **20%**
Restrictions on activities **14%**
Inability to play sports **12%**

Kids say:
Restrictions on activities **23%**
Inability to play sports **21%**
Inability to run **14%**

Source: SRBI research for GlaxoSmithKline, U.S. Census Bureau

By Justin Dickerson and Alejandro Gonzalez, USA TODAY, 2005

tem. Medical intervention—in the form of treatment therapies—is necessary to treat the disease.

STRESS

In addition to physical treatments, emotional or social help can also be useful to an asthma patient. A person with asthma may feel tension with family members. The school or work environment may not be supportive of the necessary treatments. Some people can feel very upset about not being in control of their asthma and not knowing when the next attack will happen. Any of these situations can cause an attack. These factors all contribute to a condition generally called stress.

One way to describe stress is anything that cuts down on our

Physical and emotional stress can trigger asthma attacks. It's important for asthmatics to find healthy ways to talk with friends and family about their feelings and to find other healthy ways to manage stress.

physical or emotional comfort and security. A certain amount of stress is present in everyone's life. We need some stress to help us develop and stay interested in the world around us. But changes in our routine can become too big or come at us faster than we like. At that point, we experience a level of stress that may not be healthy. We may lose our self-confidence. Instead of rising to the challenge, we feel like running away. We panic and become so angry and frustrated that we push others away with our behavior. We may also feel like no amount of trying is going to make a situation better.

When an asthma patient is too stressed, the doctors and nurses can't treat that person efficiently. Stress can also make asthma attacks become more severe and more frequent.

Research shows that prolonged stress actually produces changes in the chemistry of the body. Long-lasting stress affects the endocrine glands. These are small organs scattered around the body that regulate many of its functions. When the body is feeling stress, the endocrine glands begin to produce too much of certain hormones. These extra hormones slow down the immune system. It's quite possible for a person under prolonged stress to be more vulnerable to catching a cold or other respiratory ailment. Colds, flu, and bronchitis tend to make asthma worse. So a person coping with asthma has another reason to feel even more stressed-out when he or she comes down with a respiratory virus.

Added doses of stress-generated hormones also cause the body's breathing rate to speed up. The airways become narrower. These asthmalike symptoms can trigger a real attack. Having too much of some hormones also affects how you think and feel. They can make you irritable or depressed. As a result of these feelings, you may also be less likely to follow your asthma treatment program.

The crying, shouting, and laughing that sometimes go along with extreme stress can actually trigger asthma attacks. These stress-related gasps of air irritate the airways. A person reacting to stress in these ways may experience shortness of breath or a tight chest, followed by a full-blown flare-up of asthma.

ASTHMA AND EMOTIONS

Investigators have been studying the chemical–physical connection between asthma and emotions. A series of experiments begun in the 1990s by doctors Beatrice Wood and Bruce Miller, psychiatrists at the State University of New York in Buffalo, provides a good example. Miller and Wood asked a group of children with moderate to severe asthma—ages eight to seventeen years—to view the 1982 blockbuster movie *E.T., The Extra-Terrestrial*. While they watched the science-fiction movie, each child wore a collection of small electrical sensors on his or her chest plus a small probe attached to the finger of one hand. These devices were connected to monitoring machines similar to the lie detectors used in police work. The monitors continuously recorded heart and respiration rates, pulse, and the amount of oxygen circulating in the blood. These are all physical indicators that change shortly before the onset of an asthma attack.

The researchers chose *E.T.* because it tells a story that has a strong appeal to young people's emotions. The doctors focused on their subjects' reactions to three scenes: the opening minutes of the movie, in which the names of the actors and the moviemakers appear; a scene where the main human character, Elliott, becomes convinced that his beloved extraterrestrial friend, E.T., has died; and the final scene when E.T. says good-bye to Elliott and returns to his outer-space home.

As the young people in the study watched the opening credits, the machines recorded little physical reaction one way or the other. When the viewers saw the final scene in which E.T. says good-bye to Elliott, they all experienced similar small but positive changes in pulmonary and other functions. This is because they reacted with mixed feelings to those events. But when the young people saw the scene where Elliott thinks E.T. is dead—an extremely sad moment in the movie—some of the participants in the study experienced profound declines in pulmonary function. These reactions were similar to those that appear with the onset of an asthma episode. When Miller and Wood further examined their results, they found that the individuals who had the most emotional-physiological reactions to the sad scenes were almost always the same ones who had more sensitive and reactive airways in general.

It's still not clear precisely how emotional reaction and supersensitive airways are related. However, many investigators are on the trail. It's likely that the connection will soon become better understood. Meanwhile, it's clear that emotional stress can be a major factor in living with asthma. For all individuals with chronic asthma, it's important to look for ways to ease emotional pressures. Better and more open communication with friends and family are good places to begin. It is also very important that young people with asthma come to understand that they are not helpless and that they can influence their own health.

FAMILY

With or without asthma in the picture, adolescence tends to be a rocky period for everyone. Relationships with parents are changing. Rivalries among brothers and sisters are also likely to become more pronounced during teen years. Managing asthma may become more difficult, and jealousies over the amount of attention that the asthmatic child has received may surface. For all these reasons, the family's nerves can become frayed.

Guilt may also play a part in family stress. Asthmatic children and young people who were the focus of family concern for so long may begin to realize just how much their illness has impacted everyone. Parents may also have mixed feelings. They often mistakenly blame themselves for not being able to spare their children from sickness. Some react by becoming overprotective and being very reluctant to allow the asthmatic to stand on his or her own. ("No, you can't go on the class trip. What would happen if you had an attack?") Some deal with their fears by blaming the child. ("I told you you'd get sick if you stayed overnight at Laura's house. Now it's your fault that you're wheezing.")

Young people of all ages need their parents to be responsive to their conflicting desires for support and independence. And as children get older, they need to become sensitive to their parents,

Family counseling with a professional therapist can help the person with asthma, as well as that person's parents and siblings, reduce stress at home.

and siblings' struggles, too. Sometimes, the fastest and most effective route to better communication and reduced family stress is through a few sessions of family counseling with a professional therapist. This can help all families, including families dealing with asthma, work toward maintaining a loving, supportive, and healthy environment for everyone.

PANIC ATTACKS, ANXIETY, AND DEPRESSION

For people with asthma, as for anyone, extreme stress of any kind requires prompt attention. Extreme stress may lead to depression. Depression is a very low emotional state usually expressed as feelings of overwhelming helplessness, anxiety, and fatigue. It is a psychological condition that requires treatment just as much as asthma does. People who are depressed come to believe that they are isolated and that their life is just a series of "can'ts" and "don'ts." If the depressed person also has asthma, he or she may be gripped by the fear that, at any moment, a severe attack of asthma will occur. They often find it difficult to talk about their emotions, focusing more on their physical symptoms.

Depressed asthmatics may also neglect the specific details of their treatment. They may fail to take their medications because they feel it doesn't matter or that their friends and classmates are judging them negatively for their state of health. The result can become a vicious cycle—more and worse asthmatic attacks foll-owed by more fear and more depression. More education about medical treatment for asthma, coupled with professional counseling for depression, are the best ways to stop this cycle. This approach can relieve extreme stress and help the individual with asthma follow his or her treatment plan.

Panic attacks are another response to extreme stress. A panic attack is an episode of brief yet acute anxiety. Panic attacks related to asthma

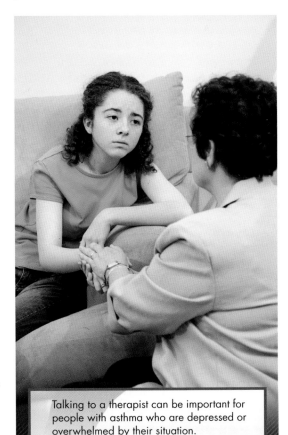

Talking to a therapist can be important for people with asthma who are depressed or overwhelmed by their situation.

www.usatoday.com

USA TODAY

Life
SECTION D

April 27, 2009

From the Pages of USA TODAY

More teens get screened

The next time you take your teen to a doctor for a physical, sports checkup or a minor illness, don't be surprised if the visit includes a little something extra: a screening for major depression.

Such screenings—in which teens answer a few questions about possible depression warning signs—are sure to become more common, thanks to a recent recommendation from the U.S. Preventive Services Task Force. The influential, independent panel, which is not connected with drug companies, doctors' groups or insurers, says routine depression screening should do more good than harm for kids ages 12 to 18.

Major depression affects more than 5% of teens and is linked with suicide, substance abuse and other serious problems. Yet it often goes undiagnosed and untreated, the panel says. (Read the full report at http://www.uspreventiveservicestask-force.org/uspstf/uspschdepr.htm.)

"If you don't ask, they won't tell," says Leslie McGuire, deputy director of the TeenScreen National Center for Mental Health Checkups at Columbia University in New York. She supports the guidelines.

But it won't be enough for doctors to just ask teens if they are depressed or to watch for outward signs, the experts say. Here's what they say a good screening should entail:

- It should be for everyone, not just clearly troubled kids. "It's something you do with a whole population to figure out who's got symptoms that might warrant a closer look," McGuire says.

- It should start with a questionnaire, on paper or a computer screen, that covers possible symptoms, such as persistent sadness, irritability and a loss of interest and pleasure in life. Several such questionnaires have been tested for accuracy.

tend to last longer and to be more severe than those experienced by people who do not have asthma. The attack usually begins with a cascade of symptoms. These can include chest pains, rapid heartbeat, sweating, trembling, and faintness. Hyperventilation—fast, shallow breathing—worsens the situation. A panic attack and

- Teens should get a chance to fill out the form in private, in the waiting room or at home before a visit. "We tell teens that moms can't peek, there's no right or wrong answer and we aren't the mental-health police," says John Genrich, a pediatrician in Colorado Springs who recently started screening patients.
- It should be scored on the spot, by the doctor or office staff. Genrich says he can score the version he uses "in about 15 seconds."
- Even if the screening raises no red flags, it should be repeated occasionally. Studies have not shown how often is ideal, but "about once a year wouldn't be unreasonable," says Ned Calonge, task force chair and chief medical officer of the Colorado Department of Public Health and Environment.
- If the screening does raise red flags (which happens about 10% of the time, McGuire says), the provider should speak with the teen to find out more, assess any immediate danger and plan next steps—including a conversation with parents. Most troubled teens "are very relieved to have somebody share this with their parents," Genrich says.
- Teens at risk should then get a full diagnostic work-up and follow-up care—which might include tests for physical problems and referrals to mental health professionals, who might then provide psychotherapy, with or without medication.

The point of screening is not to get all depressed kids on antidepressant drugs, which have real risks, Calonge says.

And it's not to get kids into pricey psychiatrists' offices, though that will be called for in some cases, says Alan Axelson, a Pittsburgh psychiatrist who has worked with the American Academy of Child and Adolescent Psychiatry and the American Academy of Pediatrics to better coordinate mental health care for kids. Axelson says some depressed kids will do well with counseling from a clinical social worker or psychologist, and all will benefit from follow-up with their pediatrician or family doctor.

But right now, many kids' doctors lack plans and support systems for treating and referring depressed youngsters, Calonge says. Those doctors, he says, should not start screening until they are better prepared to help.

—Kim Painter

an asthma attack are similar in appearance. The occurrence of one can also trigger the other. Panic attacks happen most often among people whose asthma is poorly controlled to begin with.

When a panic attack is in full swing, it is important that others remain calm. The person experiencing the panic attack needs to have his or her fears recognized rather than ignored. Recognition is the first step to regaining a sense of safety and self-assurance.

One effective measure to deal with hyperventilation is breath-coaching. A calm person reaches for the hands of the person experiencing the panic attack while demonstrating deep, slow breathing. The calm person asks the individual to breathe along in rhythm. This makes the person more conscious of what is going on. It can often help slow down the person's breathing. Once the attack has passed, it

Panic attacks and asthma attacks are frightening. Breathing can be difficult in both cases, and one type of attack can lead to the other. Breath-coaching with a calm person is one way to manage the rapid breathing often associated with a panic attack.

is important to talk about what particular event may have set off the panic and to see if there are ways to prevent or better manage that event in the future. Professional counseling is another healthy step to take in managing panic and anxiety.

SUPPORT GROUPS

Asthma support groups are a great way to get help with stress management. A support group is typically made up of a dozen or so people, all roughly the same age, who meet under the leadership of a counselor with medical knowledge of asthma. The support group offers members a place where people with asthma can talk with their peers. In the process, they learn from one another while having a good time. They share frustrations, complaints, anxieties, and triumphs. They learn that others have been through the same things. They also hear how their peers have overcome some challenges and reduced other familiar problems to manageable size.

Many asthma organizations can recommend support groups for asthmatics of all ages. For example, the website for the Asthma and Allergy Foundation of America lists local support groups. There are

A support group for people with asthma can help participants talk about their frustrations and challenges while connecting with peers.

USA TODAY

also groups for family members and caregivers. Most members of a support group work together to come up with successful strategies for managing real-life situations for their age groups. They discuss finding comfortable ways to fit in socially while dealing responsibly with their health.

Asthma summer camps offer another opportunity for young people to learn how to live with asthma. Campers enjoy all the usual summer camp activities, from swimming and tennis to adventure hikes and crafts. They have the added benefit of having fun under the supervision of a unique team of physicians, nurses, and respiratory therapists. The counselors also know about asthma firsthand. Young people who have never had a chance to be away from home on their own because of their asthma learn a greater measure of self-reliance while having a lot of fun and fresh air.

Children at an asthma camp learn methods to regulate their breathing. Asthma camps are a great place for children to meet other people living with asthma.

Asthma and allergy camps typically offer one- to two-week sessions. Almost every state in the country has camping organizations. Groups like the American Lung Association help to keep the cost of attending the camps low. Most asthma camps offer generous scholarships to individuals who qualify.

Support can also be found online. Research hospitals and organizations such as the American Lung Association offer online support groups and other resources for people with asthma and allergies. See the Resources section at the back of this book for contact information to help you get started.

CHAPTER SIX

THE FUTURE OF ASTHMA

J ulio, a thirteen-year-old student, has mild persistent asthma. He is currently on daily preventive medication and uses a rescue inhaler when necessary. Julio does a good job of taking his medication and avoiding his allergic triggers, but he wanted to do more to control his asthma without taking additional medication. His asthma doctors suggested an alternative therapy called biofeedback. Through careful training and practice with a biofeedback specialist, Julio works on controlling things like his breathing and muscle tension. Slowly, he is learning how relaxation and careful control can help to open his airways and prevent some of his asthma attacks.

Mainstream Western medicine has come a long way in treating asthma. However, it still does not have all the answers. The National Institutes of Health readily acknowledges this. It also recognizes the usefulness of hundreds of alternative remedies. These remedies have had surprising value in treating some types of asthma. The NIH is working with medical researchers to conduct scientific studies on these methods of treatment.

ACUPUNCTURE

Acupuncture is part of an ancient system of medicine that originated more than 2,500 years ago in China. Traditional acupuncture is based on the principle that a life force or energy known as chi circulates within the body. Good health is believed to occur when the energy flows through the body in a balanced and harmonious manner. The energy flows along a series of invisible meridians, or pathways, that connect the body's many organs and systems.

Acupuncturists also believe that health problems—asthma included—come as the result of interruptions or diversions of the body's energy flow. The objective of the acupuncturist is to restore the flow of energy to its proper pathways. This is done by inserting extremely thin stainless-steel needles at several of the more than 365 select points along the meridians. (Some modern acupuncturists believe that the number of points may be as great as two thousand.) The needles are then rotated gently into place. Patients describe the procedure as nearly painless.

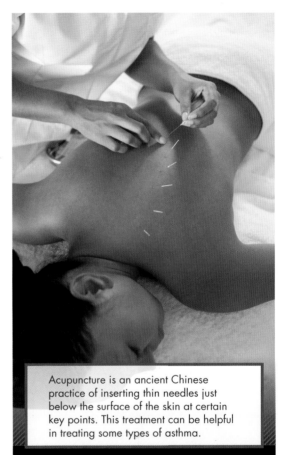

Acupuncture is an ancient Chinese practice of inserting thin needles just below the surface of the skin at certain key points. This treatment can be helpful in treating some types of asthma.

Acupuncture has been shown to be effective in reducing the pain associated with many physical and emotional conditions. This could be from the stimulation of the needles, which causes the brain to release natural chemicals known as endorphins. Endorphins are already known to be natural painkillers. When released from the pituitary gland and the hypothalamus in the brain, endorphins move into the bloodstream. They then circulate throughout the body to provide pain relief at nerve endings. Endorphins also are thought to be involved in controlling the body's reaction to stress, which is often associated with asthma attacks.

Specific acupuncture treatment for asthma involves the insertion of needles at specific points along the lung meridian. Needles can also be inserted on the back, chest, and hands to relieve coughing and other symptoms. Acupuncturists report that they have the best success with allergy-based asthma. They say that acupuncture treatments lower the individual's sensitivity to some allergens. Acupuncture can also work well in relieving general stress. It is important to remember that acupuncture should only be performed by a trained and licensed professional.

HOMEOPATHY

Homeopathy is a form of holistic medicine. The term *holistic* refers to the belief that illness is never localized in just one bodily organ or even in a single body system. Instead, it involves the whole person—mind as well as body. (In this way, holistic medicine is similar to acupuncture.) In homeopathy, symptoms are seen as positive signs that the body is trying to defend itself against an underlying disease. Rather than trying to suppress symptoms, the holistic practitioner may actually encourage their expression. Homeopathic treatment also takes into account such factors as personality and emotional makeup in selecting medications and therapies.

Perhaps the most distinctive feature of homeopathy is the way practitioners prepare and apply medications. Homeopathy teaches that the most effective drugs are those selected according to the "law of similars." Samuel Hahnemann (1755–1843) was a German physician and chemist who first formalized homeopathy in the early 1800s. He believed that the effectiveness of a drug lies in its ability to produce the same symptoms as the disease it is treating. Conventional medicine, or allopathy, teaches that substances that oppose symptoms (antibiotics, anti-inflammatories, and antihistamines, for example) offer the best hope for cure.

Hahnemann taught his followers to use medications—ranging from herbal preparations to snake venom—in very small, extremely diluted doses. In this way, he believed they were able to stimulate the body's

German physician Samuel Hahnemann (1755–1843) was an early homeopath. This type of medical treatment uses small doses of diluted substances to treat symptoms and is still practiced in modern times for many ailments, including asthma.

own self-healing mechanisms without doing any harm, no matter how toxic they might be in larger doses.

Some of the herbal treatments used by modern homeopaths in the treatment of asthma include extracts of plants and of animal organs, particularly the endocrine glands. In some instances, asthma patients take as many as fifty different extracts a day on the theory that the extracts will eventually produce immunity to the allergenic triggers. Homeopaths claim that improvements can be expected only after many months, due to the subtlety of the low-dose treatment. As with any alternative treatment, you should talk to your primary-care doctor before stopping or changing your current asthma treatment.

March 22, 2007

From the Pages of USA TODAY

Alternative medicine can play a role in allergy treatment, but researchers urge caution

Most mornings, Dominic, 8, Gabe, 7, and Ali, 5, Corradino sit munching their organic oatmeal in their kitchen in Akron, Ohio, while their mother, Tegan, doles out vitamins, fish oil pills and nettle drops. She hopes the supplements and regular visits to an acupuncturist and chiropractor will help ease their allergies and asthma.

Corradino has seasonal allergies, too, and used to pop antihistamines when needed. But it wasn't until she became a mother that she considered trying alternatives to the drug store treatments. "I worried a lot about side effects from some of the prescription drugs, so I started exploring options."

Almost 40% of Americans try some form of alternative medicine, the Asthma and Allergy Foundation of America says. Doctors say a growing number of the 35.9 million Americans who have seasonal allergies are inquiring about or already dabbling with alternative treatments as diverse as herbal teas laced with local honey, acupuncture and biofeedback.

Opinion varies among doctors on whether complementary alternative medicine can help relieve allergy symptoms. But all agree: People should not abandon their standard medications.

"Anyone with moderate to severe

HERBAL MEDICINE

Herbal medicine is based on the use of plant remedies to treat disease. It is among the oldest forms of medicine, having been practiced thousands of years ago among cave-dwelling peoples and in later ancient cultures around the world. Herbalism has enjoyed a good reputation in the evolution of Eastern and Western medical theory for thousands of years. Much of what we know in the twenty-first century allergies and asthma should absolutely remain on standard, conventional forms of medication. Asthma in particular is a potentially life-threatening condition, especially in children," says Barak Gaster, associate professor of medicine at the University of Washington.

Gaster says that in general, alternative treatments are safe and have few side effects. "But they also tend to be somewhat less effective."

Though some studies show that some alternative therapies, such as acupuncture and probiotics, may help patients with allergies, most of the studies are small and are done outside the USA.

"There is not good, rigorous scientific research showing that they are effective and safe for allergies and asthma," says Michael Zacharisen, associate professor at The Medical College of Wisconsin in Milwaukee.

Natural practitioners and physicians alike recommend consulting with a board-certified doctor before embarking on an alternative regimen. "Some common herbs typically used for allergies do have contraindications [side effects] for some people," says herbalist Erin Minehart of Belvedere, Vt.

Some people with plant allergies may be allergic to the herbs they want to take, Zacharisen says. Dangerous side effects and drug interactions could occur, too. He adds that vitamins and herbal products are considered food supplements, which do not have to be approved by the Food and Drug Administration before going on the market.

Therapies like massage and yoga hold few risks and may help, even though research has not proven their medical benefits. "If they make a person feel better, help them breathe more easily, we'd be doing a disservice if we just say phooey," Zacharisen says.

Corradino says she still relies on standard drugs when her boys' asthma is severe. "It's a journey, and I don't really know if what we're trying works. I just know they are running around, not restricted in any way. That's what's important."

—*Mary Brophy Marcus*

about modern drugs stems from the observations and experiments of early healers, herbalists, and doctors using plant potions. Some of the best asthma medications used in modern mainstream medicine are, in fact, derived from plants. These plants have long been recognized for their ability to relieve the symptoms of asthma. Examples are cromolyn, derived originally from an Egyptian weed, and ephedrine, developed from a chemical found in Chinese ephedra, or *mahuang*.

Tea made from the ephedra plant *(left)* and an herb called elecampane *(right)* are two treatments that herbalists may suggest for treating asthma.

Unlike conventional doctors, herbalists prefer to use natural compounds as they are found in nature. By contrast, conventional medicine usually extracts the chemicals from the plants or creates artificial compounds to match the plant chemicals. Herbalists also tend to mix (and frequently collect) their materials within hours of preparing a treatment. They place a great deal of emphasis on the treatment's fresh-from-nature character.

A number of herbal treatments are available for treating asthma. One is an antidote for excess bronchial mucus. It is made from wild sunflower or from an herb called elecampane. It has been used since the time of the ancient Greeks and Romans. Another is stinging nettle. For hundreds of years, many herbalists have declared that its roots and leaves help to open the airways. Stinging nettle is still widely used in Australia. People there drink the juice of this plant mixed with honey or sugar to relieve bronchial congestion, hay fever, and asthma. Herbalists also prescribe *mahuang* (ephedra) tea to clear up mucus and open clogged breathing passages. Other herbs that are believed to have a favorable effect on asthma are the leaves of the ginkgo tree and licorice, both of which are administered in herbal extracts.

Many of these herbal medications contain strong natural chemicals. It can be extremely dangerous to mix them with standard asthma medications. Another difficulty with herbal remedies is that they are difficult to standardize. Plants grown in different locations in different soils under different conditions of sun and rain, and then prepared by herbalists according to their own recipes, can have distinctly different and often unpredictable effects. Be sure to consult with your asthma doctors before pursuing herbal treatments.

RELAXATION THERAPIES

Relaxation therapies take many forms and arise from many different traditions, some even older than acupuncture. They all share the goal of calming the individual physically and emotionally. They can be safely practiced as complementary therapy so long as you continue to follow your physician's asthma treatment program faithfully.

The most ancient relaxation therapy is yoga, which was developed in India as a spiritual practice some three thousand years ago. Yoga is a holistic system that helps the individual develop physical and mental self-discipline. Yoga poses are excellent for relieving stress and improving overall physical condition. Most important for asthmatics, yoga training emphasizes control of breathing, which

Practicing yoga is a great way to control breathing and reduce stress.

is a form of life energy. Yogic breathing involves a variety of techniques and can greatly relieve stress.

Meditation is another ancient technique yoga teaches. This practice of calming the mind and body can actually slow down brain activity for brief periods. It reduces the flow of certain chemicals associated with anxiety. Practiced regularly, yoga can help improve breathing and relieve stress. Both of these can help during asthma flare-ups.

Regular practice of the physical training and meditation aspects of Chinese tai chi—a slow and gentle martial art form—can help a person with asthma focus on relaxing and breathing better. Hypnotherapy is another form of relaxation therapy. It is particularly directed at relaxing the mind. A person who is hypnotized is able to relax and focus intently on a particular subject or emotion. This makes it a useful technique in helping people overcome fears and unhealthy lifestyles such as smoking. Hypnosis has also been shown to be helpful with allergies and asthma. It gives some people a tool to relieve stress.

Massage therapy, Alexander technique, and reflexology are other alternative or complementary therapies that seek to provide relief from stress. While they are not specific to asthma, some people with chronic asthma and other respiratory problems find relief in these therapies.

BIOFEEDBACK TRAINING

Biofeedback is based on the way our bodies naturally self-adjust throughout the day. A good example of natural biofeedback is seen in the signals that our brain sends to our heart when

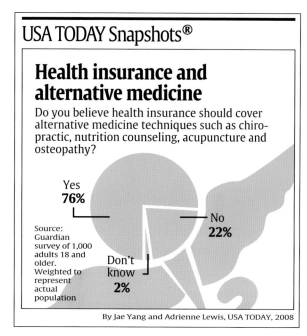

USA TODAY Snapshots®

Health insurance and alternative medicine

Do you believe health insurance should cover alternative medicine techniques such as chiropractic, nutrition counseling, acupuncture and osteopathy?

Yes
76%

No
22%

Don't know
2%

Source: Guardian survey of 1,000 adults 18 and older. Weighted to represent actual population

By Jae Yang and Adrienne Lewis, USA TODAY, 2008

we awaken from sleep and prepare to stand up. As we move from a horizontal (lying down) to a vertical (standing) position, sensors tell the heart that it must work harder. The heart accommodates by speeding up. In a short time, blood pressure increases and more oxygen becomes available. If we stand too quickly, however, the feedback mechanism cannot complete its work in time and we become dizzy.

Another example of biofeedback is found in the way we maintain balance. Various sensors in our eyes, ears, brain, and the muscles that control our skeletal frame cooperate. As our weight shifts,

A biofeedback trainer attaches recording instruments to a patient's neck that measure stress factors such as pulse rate and body temperature. By working with a biofeedback trainer, a person can learn to better recognize and manage stress triggers. This can be a helpful tool in living with asthma.

the sensors tell the body how to adjust various parts to keep from falling over.

Formal biofeedback training was developed in the 1960s. It aims to train people to use these same unconscious mechanisms in a conscious, intentional way. To do this, a biofeedback trainer connects the patient to recording instruments that measure stress-responsive factors such as pulse rate, blood pressure, body temperature, and muscle tension. The patient, who relaxes in a chair with a collection of sensors pasted on his or her skin, receives instantaneous "feedback" on the bodily changes the sensors pick up. The feedback may come in the form of flashing lights, sounds on an amplifier, or needle movements on a dial. They show high and low points of whatever is being monitored.

With coaching, the patient becomes able to relate these movements and sounds to subtle changes in his or her body. With practice, the patient learns to exert conscious influence over them through relaxation techniques. When biofeedback training was first introduced, researchers predicted that it would be possible for an asthmatic to learn to control the muscles that surround the bronchi and bronchioles to reduce airway constriction. But these hopes have mostly been abandoned. Still, biofeedback continues to be a good way to train people to relax. As relaxation helps us deal with stress, such techniques can have a useful place in asthma treatment.

NATUROPATHY AND DIET

Naturopathy is a form of alternative medicine based on the idea that disease is due to an accumulation of toxins or pollutants in the body. Collections of symptoms show the body's attempt to rid itself of these substances. Naturopaths believe that health can be regained by avoiding artificial and unnatural substances in the environment, especially in the foods we eat.

Asthmatics are sometimes found to be allergic to one or more foods. Avoidance of these foods can significantly reduce the chances of triggering some kinds of asthma attacks. But naturopaths also are on the lookout for things like too much salt in the diet, food-coloring agents, preservatives, or flavor enhancers. Foods that are fresh and unprocessed are generally more nutritious than junk foods or packaged foods. Little scientific proof is available, though, to prove that naturopathic diets will help reduce asthma symptoms. As with any alternative or complementary medicine, only time—and a lot of carefully controlled scientific studies—will settle the question.

LOOKING TO THE FUTURE

Asthma will be with us for the foreseeable future, and the number of people who have asthma continues to increase. This may be because more people live in circumstances that expose them to environmental triggers. On the positive side, some very promising advances lie on the horizon. Medical researchers are learning more about the underlying causes of asthma and how to manage the disease with greater success. Pharmacologists, experts in developing drugs, are constantly improving the effectiveness of the medications used to control inflammation and broncho constriction. Family doctors and medical specialists, the people on the front line of asthma control, are working with more urgency than ever before to identify asthma at its earliest stages.

Researchers are getting to understand the underlying causes of asthma *before* allergens trigger symptoms, *before* airways become inflamed, *before* breathing passages tighten up, and *before* mucus clogs the airways. One way medical scientists think they can do this is by taking precise

A scientific researcher prepares slides for research on allergies and allergy treatments. Better understanding of allergies can improve the treatment of asthmatic patients.

aim at earlier stages of the disease. For example, new drugs block the release of one of the irritating body chemicals that contributes to the inflammation of asthma.

GENETIC ENGINEERING

Researchers believe that it will eventually be possible to test if an unborn baby is likely to develop asthma later on. With this information, they may be able to take precautions at a very early stage of development. This would protect babies at risk from the substances that will make them sensitive to asthma. Once the cause is known, it may also be possible to repair the genes themselves.

Asthma appears to involve defects in several genes. Researchers at the Washington University School of Medicine in St. Louis, Missouri, have already tracked down one mutant gene that appears to make people more susceptible to allergies leading to asthma. The presence of this gene alone has been shown to increase the likelihood of developing allergies by ten times. Few have any doubts that many more such factors will be found. About a dozen major studies are under way to find the genes associated with asthma. So far researchers have narrowed the search to specific chromosomes where the genes thought to play a role in asthma hypersensitivity are located.

One of the most ambitious searches is being spearheaded by the National Heart, Lung, and Blood Institute, based in Maryland. Called the Collaborative Study on the Genetics of Asthma, the search involves 140 families with at least two asthmatic siblings. The families are drawn from three ethnic groups: whites, African Americans, and Hispanics. The hope is that by studying these groups in detail, the asthma genes and their particular differences, if any, will eventually reveal themselves.

Another very intriguing study involves the cooperative work of two pharmaceutical companies and a private American research foundation. Their researchers are looking for clues to the genetic basis of asthma among the inhabitants of the South Atlantic island of Tristan da Cunha. This is a British territory located in the Atlantic Ocean, halfway between South Africa and Brazil. The island's total population is only three hundred people, and nearly one-third of them have asthma. Tristanians also have exceptionally well-documented family trees, or charts of who descended from whom. These date from 1817, when the island was first settled by a handful of British colonists. Within such a tight community, it is much easier to trace how various characteristics have been passed on from one generation to the next.

Tristan da Cunha (below) is an island in the South Atlantic Ocean. By studying families in this tightly knit community where almost 60 percent of the population has some evidence of asthma, scientists hope to better understand the genetic basis for asthma.

GENETIC THERAPY

How will we use genetic information when it is found? The expectation is that it will become possible to cure asthma in a couple of ways. One will be to reach into the individual's genetic package and actually replace the asthma-causing genes with healthy genes.

Another method of genetic therapy proposed for the future involves leaving the defective genes in place but making them behave differently. Genetic engineers believe they will be able to "turn off" or "turn on" genes.

Genetic therapy for asthma is still many years away from becoming a practical reality. Not only is it very difficult to do, but there are many ethical, legal, and safety questions that have to be settled first. In the United States, the National Institutes of Health is working closely with leaders to come up with guidelines that will help ensure responsible genetic engineering.

In the twenty-first century, asthma ranks as the leading chronic disease of childhood in the United States. It's safe to say that it will continue to be the focus of some of the best research talent that science and medicine can offer for years to come. Who knows what the future of asthma treatment may hold?

GLOSSARY

acute: something that develops suddenly

allergen: any substance that causes allergic symptoms

allergy: an inappropriate or exaggerated response by the immune system to substances that, in the majority of people, cause no symptoms

alveoli: air sacs, located in the lungs at the tips of bronchioles, which hold and transfer oxygen to the bloodstream

anaphylaxis: a severe allergic reaction that must be treated quickly with medication; can be life-threatening

antibody: a protein that develops in response to a foreign substance (antigen)

antigen: a substance that can trigger an immune response, resulting in an asthmatic reaction

asthma: a chronic, inflammatory lung disease characterized by recurrent obstructed breathing

beta-adrenergic drugs: oral and inhaled drugs that quickly open constricted airways, easing wheezing and asthma attacks; also known as beta-agonists

bronchi: two main branches of the trachea that bring air into the lungs

bronchioles: small air passages that branch from the bronchi and terminate in the alveoli

bronchitis: inflammation, caused by viruses, of the bronchi

broncho constriction: a narrowing of the bronchioles; the opposite of bronchodilation

bronchodilation: a widening of the bronchioles; the opposite of broncho constriction

bronchospasm: a tightening of the muscles around airways, making them narrower

chlorofluorocarbons (CFCs): chemical agents that, when released into the air, can cause environmental damage. CFCs in metered-dose inhalers are gradually being replaced with alternative propellants.

chronic: long-term or continuous

corticosteroid: a synthetic, cortisone-like drug used to treat asthma

dander: a common allergen composed of tiny particles of dead skin, including the skin of dogs and cats and other warm-blooded pets

desensitization: the decrease in reaction to various allergens achieved through immunotherapy

dust mites: microscopic insectlike organisms that live in bedding, upholstered furniture, rugs and carpeting, and curtains. Dust mites are a major cause of asthma-related allergies.

environmental triggers: chiefly smog, smoke, air pollutants, pollen, and mold spores that start asthma attacks

episode: another word for an asthma attack or "flare-up"

exercise-induced asthma (EID): a form of asthma triggered specifically by physical activity

flare-up: another word for an asthma episode or attack

food allergy: body reactivity to either a food or a food additive

gastroesophageal reflux: a backward flow of material from the stomach to the esophagus, usually associated with lying down. Reflux causes irritation in the bronchi, which can lead to a bronchospasm.

histamine: one of the major chemical irritants, released along airways by cells, that is responsible for asthma symptoms

hypersensitivity: extreme sensitivity to substances that can cause asthmatic symptoms in the body

hyperventilation: very rapid and shallow breathing that can trigger an asthma episode

immune system: the many-faceted system that protects the body against disease and infection. When the immune system is overly active, it can lead to asthma and other allergic responses through its inflammatory response and the production of antibodies.

immunoglobulin E (IgE): the antibody primarily involved in allergic reactions

immunotherapy: a lengthy course of treatment involving allergy shots and injections for the purpose of desensitizing a patient to specific allergens

inflammation: swelling, redness, heat, and pain produced in tissue because of an irritant. Inflammation of the airways is the primary symptom of asthma.

irritant: a substance that provokes inflammation and broncho constriction in the airways

leukotriene pathway inhibitor (LPI): a drug that interferes with the production of histamines and mucus, reducing airway irritation

lung function test: an important diagnostic test used to detect the severity of asthma

metered-dose inhaler (MDI): a pocket-size canister and mouthpiece containing asthma medication under pressure. MDIs are used to deliver bronchodilation medications to the airways.

mucus: a sticky fluid produced along the airways. Mucus normally serves to lubricate the air we breathe and to trap tiny foreign particles for removal through coughing. Excess mucus, as in asthma, can plug the airways and lead to difficulty in breathing.

nebulizer: a small air compressor used to deliver medication when a metered-dose inhaler is not appropriate

peak flow meter: an inexpensive tool for obtaining daily measures of lung function

pollen: a fine, powderlike material produced by the flowering part of some plants. Pollen is a common asthma trigger.

pulmonary function test: a series of tests used to measure the capacity of suspected asthmatic lungs as compared with that of normal lungs

pulmonologist: a doctor who specializes in diseases and dysfunctions of the respiratory system

respiratory system: the group of organs, including airways and lungs, that are responsible for carrying oxygen from the air to the bloodstream and for expelling the waste product carbon dioxide

skin test: a test in which tiny amounts of allergen extracts are scratched into or applied to the surface of the skin to determine the presence of an allergenic reaction

spacer: a tubelike device that attaches to the mouthpiece of a metered-dose inhaler to aid in the dispersal of the inhalant mist

spirometer: an instrument for measuring the amount of air entering and leaving the lungs

stress: any pressure, physical or emotional, that causes emotional or psychological discomfort

trachea: the tube connecting the back of the mouth to the bronchial tree

trigger: a factor that causes an asthmatic reaction to begin

twitchy: very sensitive or easily excited

wheeze: a high-pitched whistling sound made when breathing during an asthma episode. Wheezing is the result of narrowed airways and restricted lung function.

RESOURCES

Allergy & Asthma Network/Mothers of Asthmatic (AANMA)
2751 Prosperity Avenue, Suite 150
Fairfax, VA 22031
(800) 878-4403 • http://www.aanma.org

The Allergy & Asthma Network/Mothers of Asthmatics (AANMA) is a nonprofit organization dedicated to asthma, allergies, and other related conditions. They provide education, outreach, and advocacy to call attention to and relieve the suffering of people with asthma and related conditions.

American Academy of Allergy, Asthma & Immunology (AAAAI)
555 East Wells Street
Milwaukee, WI 53202
(800) 822-2762 • http://www.aaaai.org

American Academy of Allergy, Asthma & Immunology (AAAAI) represents medical and research professionals interested in the treatment of allergies and asthma. The organization provides resources for those who treat patients with allergy, asthma, and immune issues.

American College of Allergy, Asthma & Immunology
85 West Algonquin Road, Suite 550
Arlington Heights, IL 60005
(847) 427-1200 • http://www.acaai.org

This organization was founded to bring together health professionals interested in the future of allergy and asthma treatment. Through sharing of resources and ideas, the goal of the organization is to help professionals find the best and newest ways to help their patients.

American Lung Association
61 Broadway, 6th Floor
New York, NY 10006
(800)–LUNG–USA • http://www.lungusa.org

Through education, advocacy, and research, this leading organization works to help the public improve lung health and prevent lung diseases. The site offers access to information about support groups and other helpful resources.

Asthma and Allergy Foundation of America
1233 20th Street N.W., Suite 402
Washington, DC 20036
(202) 466–7643 • http://www.aafa.org

At its website, this foundation has links to support groups, helpful educational resources, and information for clinics and specialists. The foundation also has an "Ask the Allergist" feature for people with questions about allergies.

National Heart, Lung, and Blood Institute
Information Center
P.O. Box 30105
Bethesda, MD 20824–0105
(301) 592–8573 • http://www.nhlbi.nih.gov/about/naepp/

The National Heart, Lung, and Blood Institute's National Asthma Education and Prevention Program was created to address asthma issues in the United States. Members of the program work with educators, health professionals, and other community organizations around the country to educate the public about asthma.

SELECTED BIBLIOGRAPHY

Balch, James F., and Mark Stengler. *Prescription for Natural Cures*. Hoboken, NJ: John Wiley & Sons, 2004.

Bernard, Alfred, Marc Nickmilder, Catherine Voisin, and Antonia Sardella. "Impact of Chlorinated Swimming Pool Attendance on the Respiratory Health of Adolescents." *Pediatrics*. September 14, 2009. http://pediatrics.aappublications.org/cgi/content/abstract/peds.2009-0032v1/ (April 4, 2010).

McPhee, Stephen J. and Maxine A. Papadakis, ed., *Current Medical Diagnosis & Treatment 2010*. New York: McGraw Hill, 2010.

MedlinePlus. "Asthma in Children." *NIH*, March 30, 2010. http://www.nlm.nih.gov/medlineplus/asthmainchildren.html/ (April 5, 2010).

National Institutes of Health and Friends of the National Library of Medicine. "Childhood Asthma: A Chance to Heal." *NIH MedlinePlus 2* (Fall 2007): 18–19.

National Jewish Health. "Asthma: Lifestyle Management." http://www.nationaljewish.org/healthinfo/conditions/asthma/lifestyle-management/tools/peak-flow-meter.aspx/ (April 8, 2010).

FURTHER READING AND WEBSITES

Books

Adams, Francis V. *The Asthma Sourcebook*. New York: McGraw-Hill, 2007.

Berger, William E. *Asthma for Dummies*. Hoboken, NJ: Wiley, 2004.

——. *Living with Asthma*. New York: Facts on File, Inc., 2008.

Billitteri, Thomas J. *Alternative Medicine*. Minneapolis: Twenty-First Century Medical Library, 2001.

Bock, Kenneth, and Cameron Stauth. *Healing the New Childhood Epidemics: Autism, ADHD, Asthma, and Allergies*. Chicago: Ballantine Books, 2008.

Brynie, Faith Hickman. *101 Questions about Your Immune System*. Minneapolis: Twenty-First Century Books, 2000.

Fanta, Christopher, Lynda M. Cristiano, and Kenan Hayer. *The Harvard Medical School Guide to Taking Control of Asthma*. New York: Free Press, 2003.

Fridell, Ron. *Decoding Life: Unraveling the Mysteries of the Genome*. Minneapolis: Twenty-First Century Books, 2004.

——. *Genetic Engineering*. Minneapolis: Lerner Publications Company, 2006.

Hyde, Margaret O., and Elizabeth Forsyth, MD. *Stress 101: An Overview for Teens*. Minneapolis: Twenty-First Century Books, 2008.

Kidd, J. S., and Renee A. Kidd. *Potent Natural Medicines: Mother Nature's Pharmacy*. New York: Chelsea House, 2006.

Lew, Kristi. *The Respiratory System*. New York: Marshall Cavendish Benchmark, 2010.

Smith, Terry L. *Asthma*. New York: Chelsea House, 2008.

Tagliaferro, Linda. *Genetic Engineering: Modern Progress or Future Peril?* Minneapolis: Twenty-First Century Books, 2010.

Wohlenhaus, Kim. *Asthma Information for Teens: Health Tips about Managing Asthma and Related Concerns*. Detroit, MI: Omnigraphics, 2010.

Websites

Asthma and Allergy Foundation of America (AAFA)
http://www.aafa.org/

The AAFA seeks to improve the quality of life of people who suffer from allergies and asthma through education, advocacy, and research.

Mayo Clinic
http://www.mayoclinic.com/health/asthma/DS00021

The renowned Mayo Clinic provides an in-depth look at the causes, symptoms, and treatment of asthma.

National Institutes of Health
http://www.nhlbi.nih.gov/health/dci/Diseases/Asthma/Asthma_WhatIs.html

Read information, watch video, and follow links relating to asthma on this government-sponsored website.

TeensHealth
http://kidshealth.org/teen/

TeensHealth is a project of the Nemours Foundation, an organization established in 1936 by Alfred I. DuPont and is dedicated to improving the health and spirit of young people. Doctors and health care experts review all information before it is posted on the website.

WebMD
http://www.webmd.com/

This site allows you to search for information about thousands of health topics. It contains a section specifically devoted to asthma in teens and adults.

LERNER e SOURCE™

Expand learning beyond the printed book. Download free, complementary educational resources for this book from our website, www.lerneresource.com

INDEX

ABOUT THE AUTHOR

Wendy Murphy is a writer and editor who has written more than two dozen books in the medical and behavioral fields. She has written about such topics as nuclear medicine, the workings of the human brain, modern drug development, and the history of physical therapy. She is also the author of *Orphan Diseases: New Hope for Rare Medical Conditions* and *Weight and Health*. She lives in Connecticut.

PHOTO ACKNOWLEDGMENTS